Speak Like a President

G000075320

Speak Like a President

How to Inspire and Engage
People with Your Words

Simon Maier

A & C Black • London

First published in Great Britain 2010

A & C Black Publishers Ltd
36 Soho Square, London W1D 3QY
www.acblack.com

A CIP record for this book is available from the British Library.

ISBN: 9-781-4081-2533-5

This book is produced using paper that is made from wood grown in managed,
sustainable forests. It is natural, renewable and recyclable. The logging and
manufacturing processes conform to the environmental regulations of the country of
origin.

Design by Fiona Pike, Pike Design, Winchester
Typeset by Saxon Graphics Ltd, Derby
Printed in Great Britain by Cox & Wyman, Reading RG1 8EX

For David L. Maier

"Be kind to thy father, for when thou wert young,
Who loved thee so fondly as he?
He caught the first accents that fell from thy tongue,
And joined in thy innocent glee."

Margaret Courtney (1822–1862)

Contents

A Beginning

Wednesday Morning, New York

The roar of the crowd could be heard despite the fact that the audience was at least two hundred yards away. He guessed that the stadium was full. Maybe a hundred thousand this time? Perhaps more. He exhaled, shrugged his shoulders, and fingered his tie. The light in the narrow corridor deep below the stage area was dim, and the small LED lamps glowed quite prettily, he thought, from floor installations—strangely elaborate for what was little more than a very large cellar. The three Secret Service agents looked as if they were auditioning for a low-key horror movie; apart from their well-lit chins, they were making him feel a little claustrophobic now by standing too close. Two wore sunglasses, and the one who didn't was staring above the senator's head. He seemed to be listening.

The senator's make-up artist had just left, and his scriptwriter was following her, walking down the corridor twirling his car keys and whistling a Green Day song. He snapped open his cell phone to call his friend (not a girlfriend, as he kept telling people) Sally Shoesmith, a mainstream ad agency business development manager in London. He knew that Sally wanted to know how the tour was going. She also had to do something about her Wednesday morning sales meetings, and she wanted some help from the young scriptwriter. One of the agents looked at the receding back of the jaunty figure and then at his watch. He put up a hand and showed four fingers to the senator. The noise from the crowd dulled a little while someone made a muffled announcement. There was a slight pause, a receding sea, a heartbeat, and then a huge welling up of a tsunami roar. The senator wondered if they'd still cheer like this after his first year in office. Maybe. Maybe not. He stopped pacing, shrugged his shoulders again, sipped water from a plastic cup, glanced up at the bright blue and red water pipes, and then focused straight ahead. The agents formed a phalanx around him. He put the cup down, shot his cuffs, smiled to no one (just giving his facial muscles a run, he thought), and they all began walking as one along the corridor toward the open door.

"Showtime," said the scriptwriter, who was waiting for the senator at the edge of the bright light. The wordsmith had failed to get hold of Sally Shoesmith, although he'd forgotten to turn his phone off. The roar was now huge and the sun blinding. The senator heard the beginning of his introduction. He looked into the eyes of the scriptwriter and smiled genuinely while patting the young man's back twice. The young man returned the smile and felt happy. "It's all good, sir. Good to go." A pause and then he shouted over the noise, "Speak like a president!"

Introduction

"If I could just find the right words..."
Barack Obama, *Dreams from My Father*, 1995

Barack Obama was thirty-four in 1995 when he wrote *Dreams from My Father*. He had only recently completed his law degree and, as a result of becoming the first African-American president of the *Harvard Law Review*, had been invited to write a memoir. The book was modest in its ambition and published to soft, if not effusive, reviews. Who knows if anyone had thought that this young man would become famous? The book sold in reasonable numbers and then more or less disappeared, although obviously that position has changed considerably since. It's a personal and seemingly unguarded book. After all, at the time, the young lawyer had no idea what was to happen thirteen years later. In the book he describes his memories of the month he had spent, as a schoolboy, with the father who had lived for most of his life on another continent. The main thing that struck the boy was the way his father talked: "Whenever he spoke... his large hands outstretched to direct or deflect attention, his voice deep and sure, cajoling and laughing—I would see a sudden change take place in the family...It was as if his presence had summoned the spirit of earlier times." His father's voice had a strong influence on the future president.

Obama made his first political speech while still in college. He was asked to introduce a small anti-apartheid rally. The audience numbers were modest. He describes it as a crowd of "a few hundred restless after lunch." As he waited to speak, Obama recalled "the power of my father's words to transform. If I could just find the right words, I had thought to myself. With the right words everything could change—South Africa, the lives of ghetto kids just a few miles away, my own tenuous place in the world." He went up to the stage, he writes, "in a trancelike state." Afterward, people came up to Obama and said that there were lines and messages in his speech that they would always remember.

What great speakers say is remembered. Good or bad. When, in January 2009, Obama spoke for the first time as the 44th president of the United States of America, billions of people listened and watched as he asked for, and offered, change. Well, the jury's out on the politics and the change he demanded, then offered. Some claim to be disappointed; others comment that what he inherited will take time to repair. Still others say that his inaugural wasn't his best speech, and that may be so, but listen to or indeed read any of his speeches and you will find the ebb and flow of fluent language along with the presentation and reiteration of messages vital, striking, and memorable. Speaking in public is clearly a political necessity for Obama, as it is for many in business, education, and politics (although, by the results, sometimes you really wouldn't think so). For Obama it seems also to be a personal need. He's a superb orator, and he also consciously puts oratory and rhetoric right at the heart of his political being and, in so doing, will embed himself in a vital American tradition. But, of course, throughout the world—including on occasion in the US—many politicians and business leaders are woefully clumsy in the answers to specific questions, and awkward and unclear in their explanations. Their grammar is usually all over the place and, while that may not matter elsewhere and in a social setting, it *does* matter if the result is meant to aid understanding and clarity. Or to get the viewer or listener to buy into their argument or proposition. The rhetoric, the way with words, the persuasive language—are often missing.

The history of the American republic is one that can be traced through its rhetoric: "Four score and seven years ago our fathers brought forth on this continent," "Ask not what your country can do for you," "Ich bin ein Berliner," "I have a dream," "It's morning in

America." We can all recite one or two famous lines of American rhetoric and that must indicate something. And, similarly, we all know one or two lines from Churchill and just maybe some of you may know a few lines from the likes of George Washington, Patrick Henry, Nehru, Ghandi (Mahatma and Indira, although no relation), Pericles, Aristotle, Mao, Cicero or perhaps even Hitler. Great speeches are memorable as are the phrases and repetitions that populate them. And the fact is that with practice and rehearsal, it's not just presidents who can make a great speech, so can you.

This book was written because there is a dearth of great oratory, and great oratory can still move hearts and minds. Not just political hearts and minds or even those that need refreshment in the world of commerce, but hearts and minds in any scenario where a great speech will make a difference to the way people think. When you hear a great speech, you know that you've heard a great speech, but they are rare. Great speeches have passion. Passion is a driver, whether it's passion about sales figures or passion about trying to put right a mighty wrong. But great speeches rarely just "happen." Speechmaking takes skill and practice, understanding and thought, confidence, knowledge and an ability to present an argument. People in all walks of life complain that they have little time to prepare speeches. But time spent learning more effective oral communication skills is perhaps one of the best investments you can make, whether you're a politician, business executive, coach, parent, academic, entertainer, or a boss. This book is written to touch the best of your ability and to make you better aware of the possibilities of speaking like a leader, of speaking like a president.

Chapter One
Whatever You Say

"Believe me, it is not failing to speak out with promptitude and energy that is the matter with you; it is having nothing consistent or valuable to say."
Matthew Arnold (1822–1888)

The greatest presidents—along with a few religious leaders, some politicians, a number of political leaders, and a handful of business chiefs—have tended to be remembered as the greatest speakers. One of the reasons for this (other than media profile) is the sheer quality of writing. While the content of Obama's books might be a little thin (which actually is perhaps an unfair criticism because they are of course now a fascinating insight), his writing style is congruent with the flowing language of his speeches. Obama takes a close interest in the language and content of what he says in public, and he works with his speechwriters, as of course he should, to ensure that they capture his particular, comfortable style. It isn't a lazy style, but one which sounds natural and clever. On the whole, we all understand what he is saying and why; we get the emotion and the tone; we anticipate the sentences to come. In his second memoir, *The Audacity of Hope*, published in 2006, Obama describes his speechmaking capability as a "certain talent for rhetoric," and his speeches are filled, thrillingly, with the formal rhetoric of the sort that would be recognizable to the likes of Cicero*—in whose time rhetoric, along with grammar and logic, formed one-third of an education. (A

---

*   A Roman statesman, orator and writer.

fraction of that third right now would be added value indeed within any nation's educational strategies.) What Obama does on the world's stages is as old as Aristotle—whose treatise *Rhetoric* made plain the basics (the rules really) for the art of persuasion four hundred years before the birth of Christ. And it's with an understanding of rhetoric that we should start.

Rhetoric—The Beginning

Rhetoric, of which oratory is part, is the study of speech composition and delivery. It's the shaping of the words that you will speak whereas oratory is formal speechmaking. Rhetoric is the study of all available means of teaching and persuading a group of people. According to Plato (in *Phaedrus*), rhetoric is "the art of winning the soul by discourse." In overall terms, Plato had it right. Aristotle, in his *Rhetoric*, defined it this way: "Rhetoric is the faculty of observing in any given case the available means of persuasion." Cicero believed that rhetoric was all about truth. In *Tusculanarum Disputationum*, he states that, "Our minds possess by nature an insatiable desire to know the truth." And in his *De Inventione*, Cicero said, "Rhetoric is one great art comprised of five lesser arts: *inventio, dispositio, elocutio, memoria* and *pronunciatio*." Translated into English these "lesser arts" mean "invention," "arrangement," "diction," "memory," and "delivery." Invention was the discovery of the relevant material; arrangement entailed putting the materials together in a structured way; diction was concerned with finding the appropriate style of speech for a particular occasion—grand, middle, or plain (the latter sometimes known as "low"); memory gave guidance on how to remember speeches, much as an actor would do now (and, of course, there's little difference between an actor or a public speaker on stage); and delivery gave guidance on the techniques of public speaking. One can't really argue with any of this and it's as good a guideline to public speaking as any.

Public speaking comes down to personality and belief as much as anything else. Our topic is much less about "thou shalts" and "thou shalt nots" and much more about how oratory can work for you and you with it. Quintilian, whose full name was Marcus Fabius Quintilianus, was a Roman rhetorician who reinforced the general view of rhetoric by saying that, "Rhetoric is the art of speaking well." It's a simple and direct definition, and perhaps that's the main element that you must remember, but there's more to rhetoric than just that. Rhetoric is also about making a point, ensuring that the audience *gets* the point and that the point then sticks so that it is remembered long afterward. Most scholars (Edwin Black, Kenneth Burke, Stephen Toulmin, George Campbell, Edward Corbett, Robert Connors, Wayne Booth, and even the wonderful Marshall McLuhan, to name but a few) have agreed over time that rhetoric is the persuasive use of language. Persuasion and argument were regarded in Greek and Roman times (and actually up to the twentieth century) as necessary skills. Until the eighteenth century, the study of rhetoric was one of the central disciplines in European universities alongside theology, natural and moral sciences, and law. Persuasion and argument had to be credible, though, to be of any use.

Ethos was the name given by Aristotle to that part of rhetoric that establishes a speaker's credibility or bona fides. In other words, is he or she someone to whom you should lend an ear? Is there value in what he or she says? Can you trust his or her reputation? Do you like him or her? Is he or she actually worthy of your time? If a CEO or politician was to expect an audience of five hundred to stay put when he or she hadn't bothered to prepare or rehearse a speech about the future of the company or that of the country, his or her ethos would be zero. And, of course, you don't need to be a CEO or politician to display errant arrogance or ignorance. The actual argument—the message, the appeal, the logic—is what Aristotle called *logos*. And *pathos* was the name given by Aristotle for the manipulation of the audience's emotions, part of the speech armory often forgotten by speakers these days at all levels in politics and, particularly, in business. Manipulation doesn't of course have to be a negative. Think of the last speech you heard—any speech—when your emotions were manipulated.

Rhetoric For Today

T. S. Eliot (not always an easy writer to understand, and a reader whose flat, dull renditions of his own work put people off the verse) maintained that the meaning of a poem was something that the poet would use to distract the reader while the poem did its true job upon him or her. The same sort of thing could be said about political or business rhetoric. As rhetoricians from Aristotle down through the ages have recognized, the style and shape of an address are vital to its persuasive force. Much of the work of political (and now business) rhetoric depends on what it sounds like—or, if you want to be technical, how it "scans." Don't groan, but it's much the same as with poetry. Think of the steady, obdurate thump of stresses in Churchill's wartime mantra of "blood, toil, tears and sweat" or the perfect "music" of the opening line of the main peroration of the American Declaration of Independence: "We hold these truths to be self-evident." It's a perfectly cadenced iambic pentameter, and it soothes the soul because that's what iambic pentameters do. Here's an example from Shakespeare's prologue to *Romeo and Juliet*: "Two households, both alike in dignity, in fair Verona, where we lay our scene..." It does soothe, doesn't it?

Obama's winning slogan, "Yes we can," (about which he was initially unsure and thought far too plain) actually draws much of its strength from its three stressed syllables. It is a metrical object called a molossus—thump, thump, thump; as in Alfred Lord Tennyson's poem, "Break, Break, Break" or Seamus Heaney's "The Squat Pen Rests." You could, arguably, scan it as an anapest (which goes "diddly DUM"), but Obama doesn't. The official transcript of his speech at the New Hampshire primary punctuates it like this: "Yes. We. Can."

The Basics of Speechmaking Are Easy

Truthfully, none of the basics of making a speech are hard. It really is a question of marshaling your argument, your thesis, your proposition—the reason that you're standing there in front of people. And, much as is the case with any other skill, there are some rules and guidelines that should be followed along with a huge wealth of ideas and examples that can be gleaned from history's greatest speakers and speeches. For example, repetition, particularly in the form of anaphora (where a phrase is repeated at the beginning of successive lines), is one of the prime oratorical tools and one in which Obama, among others, revels. His speech at the Iowa caucus on January 3, 2008 began: "You know, they said this time would never come. They said our sights were set too high. They said this country was too divided, too disillusioned to ever come together around a common purpose." He went on: "I'll be a president who finally makes healthcare affordable...I'll be a president who ends the tax breaks...I'll be a president who harnesses the ingenuity...I'll be a president who ends this war in Iraq." Later, his speech used sentences beginning with "This was the moment when...this was the moment when...this was the moment when..." And, as his speech built to its peak, he stated: "Hope is what I saw...Hope is what I heard...Hope is what led a band of colonists to rise up against an empire." If you know the devices and you're brave enough to apply them to what you have to say, you're well on the way to making a good speech, if not yet a great one. And don't make the mistake of thinking you can't use devices used by presidents. As long as they're appropriate, why not?

Politicians everywhere, particularly presidents of the United States, have used such devices for a long time. But, strangely, very few business executives have ever followed suit, and few do. Maybe it's because business people think that they can make presentations without any rehearsal and little preparation or that speech preparation is not time well spent. Or perhaps it's because business executives prefer to keep emotion and numbers very separate. Or perhaps there's an embarrassment in showing too much soul. If so, that's a great shame because the power of rhetoric is plain. To an American aware of his own country's history, Obama's comforting repetitions will bring to mind (probably unconsciously) the Declaration of Independence. Interestingly, the run of charges against King George III in that extraordinary document rolls out in an unstoppable anaphoric fugue. "He has refused...He has forbidden...He has refused...He has called together...He has dissolved...He has refused." But the acute listener will also hear in Obama's oratory a deeper and older rhythm, of the psalms in the King James's version of the Bible. That flows into his language through another level of input well understood by most Americans: The rhetoric of the civil rights movement started in the Baptist churches of the southern United States. There is no shame in borrowing styles—as long as the result isn't risible. Most of the great speakers borrowed ideas, quotations, styles, and devices from others to make a new whole, to sell an idea, to convert thinking, to bring hope, to tell people something new. You can do it too. Sales figures or politics—it makes no difference. It's all about convincing people.

Rhetoric and Presidents

It is extraordinary what's been achieved in the name of communications. What is clear is that in order to convince large numbers of people unequivocally, before the advent of technology, speeches had to be consistent and excellent, clever and witty, humorous where appropriate, certainly fit for the purpose, challenging, carefully considered, and with argument that was plain. More recently, key communicators—politicians, business people, diplomats, those in education, and agitators throughout the world—have felt less of a need to make "the big speech." Sound bites, they believe, will do. But, actually, sound bites won't always do. Neither will only a tweet or a text. What is said in great speeches moves people and is remembered long after the balloons have popped or shrunk, long after the wine stain on the floor has dried, and aeons after the cheese-and-cracker crumbs have been vacuumed up. It's also no surprise to find that most American presidents have shown that oratory and powerful speeches make an enormous difference in persuasive argument. When you have a moment, take a look at Theodore Roosevelt's inaugural address (1905) and Woodrow Wilson's first inaugural address of 1913, where he described his New Freedom. Then you might glance at Franklin Delano Roosevelt's first inaugural address (1933), in which he described his New Deal. These (and others) are premier persuasions. They are speeches not just in form and substance but also in delivery and belief. They lift fears and anxieties. They promote safety and leadership. They convince.

Many presidential speeches have presented beautifully articulated propositions. And it's any speech's proposition that is the important ingredient—what you're saying, why, and what result you want. Woodrow Wilson's first inaugural not only explained what he wanted and what he meant by progress, but he also explained why such ideals and ambition were important; these things were lacking in early-twentieth-century American politics. FDR, in his first inaugural, explained the New Deal and also conquered the endemic fear that had caused paralysis during the American Depression. JFK's inaugural called upon Americans to be of service while inspiring civic idealism. The process is much like designing a TV commercial. The proposition has to be crystal clear to the creative team, and the end result (within an average of fifteen or so seconds) has to make that same proposition unequivocally clear to those millions who will watch and hear it. Setting out your position and your proposition is key. Management trainers talk about "elevator pitches." These are speeches usually made by a junior executive to a senior one in the time it takes to go from the first floor to the twentieth, for example. If you can get your message, your main point, over in that time, then you are a clear and logical thinker and, no doubt, you'll go far. Of course, in a speech you have more time, but the process is much the same.

Rhetoric and Your Position in History

Very often a speaker can gain position and respect by locating him or herself in history. You can do that too. And it doesn't have to be world history of course. The "history" can relate to a modest project or initiative, to a relationship, to a marriage, to a business, to a country, and to time. Indeed, Obama locates himself in history—a clever approach. One of his early campaign catchphrases was, "There is something happening in America." He also talks about "unyielding faith," "impossible odds," and "the voices of millions." He urges crowds to recognize that "this was the moment." Such use of the past tense gives us the odd sense of already looking back at the moment, of being in and out of time. It puts the speaker and his or her message right at the front of the audience's mind, and it shows the speech content to be very big and therefore very important—of the moment. You can do this. Try it now. Consider a sentence which begins "This was the moment when the campaign to deliver profitable returns began," or "This was the moment when the team understood that the new system worked." You'll see that it gives what you have to say (and the implication of what you have to say) great weight, even if the weight of the "thing" isn't that big a deal. *Make* it a big deal. Of course, you should make a big deal of something only if that something is important to you and, crucially, to your audience. It's all about the proposition. It's all about expanding the way people see you and hear you. It positions you as being a bigger player. But don't boast. Show instead that you have developed or achieved something big. Something of value. Then, through oratory, it's your job to tell others about this "value." State the proposition and then expand it in order to sell the idea.

Good Oratory is Rare So There's Room for You

Despite what we may see in Obama's speeches, oratory today (let alone great oratory) is rare. It's not generally taught in secondary schools and rarely in tertiary education. Certainly, debating societies exist, but they're regarded as elitist, and the process of debating isn't refined or nurtured in any particular way. This isn't just an American conundrum but an international issue. The standard of political and business "public" discourse is low everywhere. Public speaking is, by and large, ignored, resented, or avoided. Where have all our orators gone? Are there so few left? Why are there so few left? Do people really not want to listen to argument and persuasive language beautifully delivered? The social, financial, and governmental issues are as pressing and dramatic as they ever were. Perhaps even more so. The world is still regularly on the edge of something dangerous, dark, or doom-laden. These are times which in the future may well be marked as history's hinges, so where are the big vocal moments? Maybe our collective patience is less than it was. We want everything immediately and we won't wait for much. Perhaps the advent of sparkling technology is truly the core reason for the demise of dazzling oratory. We have mouthfuls of rolling news, small chunks of TV, tweets, e-mails, Web sites, Facebook, sound bites, podcasts, immediate headlines, and texts. Maybe these are sufficient. But there are times when the very short pieces of information just don't satisfy, because they don't offer the detail, persuasion, emotion, passion, charm, or argument that we sometimes need. Of course, there are blogs where we can rant and rave to our heart's content, but maybe that's not enough either. Small bits of text don't offer "voice," shades of light, dark, character, deep humor, shared wit, heartfelt persuasion, or inflection. They don't always influence or, if they do, they're not sufficiently thorough for even our impatient needs.

Deep down (and in parts of the world, not so deep down), we do genuinely thirst for the live event or its live transmission on television. We thirst for the moment when our emotions are aroused and the back of the neck tingles, when we can see a future, or when we are made to believe in something. We often want the direct rhetoric, words that persuade, encourage, calm, and give us hope, offer change, alter minds, shape opinions, explain the present, shed the past, and plan the future. When we hear it we often want more. Sometimes we want someone to echo or match our own aspirations, feelings, anger, or, unfortunately, our hate and our fears that lead to hate. Sometimes we need someone to explain company policy or a political force, a set of sales figures or a subject, with heart and passion. People still go to the theater, to the opera, to places of worship, to the movies, to rock concerts, and to sports events; people still go to where other people are, to be in the same space, to receive communication, to laugh, to be entertained. When the experience is good, people want to repeat it. There is still a need to take the collective and be together for a reason. Great speeches can still do that.

Making a Speech is Straightforward

Making a speech is straightforward—although to do so requires effort and preparation, more than is required to put together an oversimplified PowerPoint concoction. Making a *great* speech is straightforward, too, but needs practice and an absolute desire to deliver an idea, to seek change, to charge the audience to think differently, to prove a point, to close the circle of argument. There has to be a desire in you to show and tell, to convince and prove, to touch audience feelings, to tell stories to make your point, and to connect. Making this connection is what great oratory is all about. At the front of E. M. Forster's novel *Howard's End*, there is a page with two words: "Only connect." It is what all art, literature, movies, plays, actors, writers, and speakers seek—connection. That is the goal. That is the way by which persuasion, tears of gratitude, laughter at a shared moment, decisive action, and change are made to happen. As soon as people in your audience nod, as soon as they smile, as soon as they laugh, as soon as they applaud or cheer, they are in *your* world. Your job is to keep them there.

POINTS TO REMEMBER

- Rhetoric, of which oratory is part, is the study of speech composition and delivery. It's the shaping of the words that you will speak. Oratory is formal speechmaking. Rhetoric is the study of all available means of persuading people.
- Without rhetoric, presidential speeches would be nothing. Obama has rekindled the flame of oratory by using rhetoric with care and great power. You can do this too. Many presidential speeches are beautifully articulated propositions. But you can offer the same.
- The rhetoric of ancient Greece and Rome sets a great example. The principles are still pertinent today.
- When making a speech, you can position yourself in "history"— history of the company, the school, a department, the wedding. You too can say, "This was the moment when…"
- Public speaking relies on personality, but there are some language and structural rules—none of which are that difficult but, if you really want to succeed as a great orator, then you have to practice and practice.
- People like listening to flowing language in the same way they like listening to music. Content is of course very important indeed, but the sound and poetry of language are crucial as well. We can learn a great deal about rhythm and language from poetry.
- People rely on technology and TV for local, national and international information. Oratory is missing from technological methods of communication; people everywhere respond to great speeches.

Chapter Two
This Little Thing
Called Oratory

**"A speech is poetry: cadence, rhythm, imagery, sweep!
A speech reminds us that words, like children, have the
power to make dance the dullest beanbag of a heart."**
Peggy Noonan (1950–), speechwriter to President Reagan

Expansion was the great theme of Obama's election night speech in
Chicago on November 4, 2008: from the small (the local) to the
medium-sized (the national) to the huge (the global); from the single
moment of the "right now" to the great time line of history. He went
from the solidity of the 106-year life of Ann Nixon Cooper, through
the twentieth century, to the here and now, and from the segregated
and troubled South to the moon and beyond. Obama's key and
favored oratorical influence, Abraham Lincoln, marked a separate
strand in his presentation and his speaking style. He pointedly chose
to launch his campaign in the city where the great nineteenth-
century champion of the Union practiced law. Declaring his candidacy
on February 10, 2007, in Springfield, Illinois, Obama began by talking
about what the life of "a tall, gangly, self-made Springfield lawyer
tells us...He tells us that there is power in words. He tells us that there
is power in conviction...He tells us that there is power in hope."
Obama talks about how Lincoln achieved change through "his will
and his words." This is strong stuff, and such application can work in
a business setting just as much as a political one. Not only can you
talk about Lincoln achieving change (if the example is appropriate; if

not, then choose another), but you can also talk about someone like Sally Shoesmith from your business development department trying to achieve change.

Be a Performer

Obama, and many speakers like him, act the part very well. Anyone "up there" on stage is literally performing and, to get a result, the performance has to be good. The aim is to make people want to hear you speak again—whether the situation is a meeting room on the third floor with twelve sales people picking their teeth after lunch or a hundred thousand people on a hot evening in a huge park waiting with bated breath for the person who's going to hopefully lead them out of poverty or despair. All orators, all great orators, want to be heard more than once. There's no shame in this. That's what you're doing—performing, taking the stage, and acting out a drama. And you want to be wanted. You want the audience to look forward to your second appearance this time next week or whenever it is. And, lest we forget, no matter how "small" you think the presentation or speech is, this is theater, this is drama. Most actions should be orchestrated and every gesture carefully considered—not in an obscene display of unnatural or uncomfortable behavior and certainly not in a way that looks rehearsed or wooden. Everything that you do onstage, or in front of any audience, should be considered beforehand. Practice and rehearsal are truly important, despite what business colleagues and political acolytes may say to you. Acting the part on any stage (and for "stage" read anywhere where you appear in front of a group of people who are all looking at you) involves good preparation and good ideas about how to make a simple message powerful and memorable. Just like an actor. And the best actors are those who prepare carefully and seriously, who put time aside to do nothing else. That's fine for them, you'll be muttering, that's what they do for a living, but I have a business to run/ a department to manage/a wedding to organize. This is undeniably true, but communicating with your audience is what you're there to do and, if you're going to do it at all, then do it brilliantly.

Create a Reason for People to Listen to You Again

Obama, way back, understood the need to get audiences to want him to speak again and again so that they could listen to him more and more. He knew then that if it was announced that he was to appear on TV, well, he would do what it took to get people to be home to watch. He would ensure, one must assume, that he was an oratorical proposition worth his weight in viewing gold. Obama prepared. He does so still. His language is full of parallel structures, examples, and qualifying statements, not just for harmony and easiness on the ear, but to give the impression of striving for the right word, the exact idea. He uses language which means much and sounds good.

You don't have to be a lawyer, a preacher, or, indeed, a president to speak as brilliantly as a lawyer, preacher, or president. Whatever you do for a living, whatever you do day in and out, will add value in some way to your speech content and your ability to speak well, whether your speech is as a best man, as a CEO of an international bank, or as a contributor to Sally Shoesmith's sales meetings. Think about a speaker you admire, whether that's a personal friend, a member of your family, a famous politician, or a local cleric. Don't you want to hear that person speak again? Consider why you do. It's not one thing but an amalgam of several. The African American and lawyer in Obama blend with the preacher and determined spirit also in Obama. His understanding of political audience blends with his understanding of an audience that has lost hope or is in dire need of jobs. He knows what presses people's buttons. If you know what presses your audience's buttons, that's much more than half the battle won. In *The Audacity of Hope*, Obama wrote that the language of the Founding Fathers is so deeply plumbed into the American unconscious that when he was teaching law at Harvard: "Sometimes I imagined my work to be not so different from the work of the theology professors who taught across campus—for, as I suspect was true for those teaching scripture, I found that my students often felt they know the constitution without having really read it." This is perhaps unique to the United States, but every nation will have its own shared cultural reference points.

Learn From Other Orators

Obama also went (and likely still goes) out of his way to learn from other orators, from others whose ability to practice brilliant rhetoric was well known. He seeks out reasons why great orators were sought out by audiences. So must you. There is no shortcut. Again in *The Audacity of Hope*, Obama describes watching in person the way that at a lectern, George W. Bush's "easy affability was replaced by an almost messianic certainty." And by the way ladies and gentlemen, just you wait: George W. Bush will be seen in the future as a better president than he is currently, and his speeches are (for the most part) excellent. Many of them exhibit a superb rhetoric superbly delivered. For example, look at, read, or listen to his speech made to Congress on September 20, 2001: "Tonight, we are a country awakened to danger and called to defend freedom. Our grief has turned to anger and anger to resolution. Whether we bring our enemies to justice or bring justice to our enemies, justice will be done." And from the same speech, he uses clever devices to engage with the country—for example, repeating the beginning of sentences like this: "We will come together to improve...We will come together to promote...We will come together to give...We will come together to strengthen...We will come together to take." You'll recognize the device now. Now you can use it.

If you want to become a great speaker, then you must first learn about the great orators who have come before you. You must immerse yourself in their speeches, read the text, listen to recordings, and pay close attention to the turns of phrases and textual symmetries, the pauses and crescendos, the metaphors and melodies that have enabled the greatest speeches to stand the test of time. Establish what such speeches did, whether they lifted hearts when people had little hope, gave warmth during times of despair, refined the characters of men, inspired great and brave feats, gave courage to the downtrodden and exhausted, honored the dead, or changed the course of history. Listen to language on the bus, on the train, on the radio. Listen to and learn clever phrases (and make sure you understand them), and learn how a simple point is expressed simply. Listen, read, or look out for impact.

Create Impact—That's What Great Orators Do and Did

Oratorical impact is not new of course; in fact, the complete opposite is true. Throughout history, certainly as far back as ancient Greek and Roman times, men and women have given memorable speeches. We are most familiar with orators such as (in no particular order) Roosevelt, the Kennedy brothers, Reagan, Mandela, Darrow, Demosthenes, Douglass, Clinton, Churchill, Ho Chi Minh, Mussolini, MacArthur, Cicero, and the list goes on. Of course these may not necessarily be great people but they are great speakers. They approach subjects, topics, and themes in certain ways to create enormous impact and extraordinary results on a huge scale—for good or bad.

Of course, not everyone regards oratory and high rhetoric as important. Some believe that speeches are easy, and if an executive has given one or two presentations reasonably well already, then general opinion in the office will be that that the executive must be a competent speechmaker because he or she has made one before. But the process of having to give and, heaven forefend, having to prepare or, goodness gracious, having to rehearse a speech makes some people feel sick, fearful, bored, and sometimes angry. Whatever the case, few see it as an honor and a privilege. Most strangely, few see it as a golden opportunity. Oratory is indeed a conduit of opportunity. Benjamin Disraeli, that great breath of fresh air and example of intelligent oratory (who incidentally had a disastrous opening speech when he was elected to the British House of Commons in 1837) is often compared to the deliverer of dusty Victorian rhetoric, William Gladstone—himself by no means a lightweight. However, to hear the arguments and debates between them was a delight for MPs in the House of Commons. Today's British parliamentary debates tend to sound a little like a series of press releases being read out, with little thought about any interaction or about how any audience might feel or think. Any debate becomes defensive with structured disagreement or attacking dogma, not much more. Crushing denunciations, brilliant probes, emotional defenses, rallying arguments—all are by and large absent, even in the debates that, in theory, decide how the United Kingdom is run. Historians will discover what existed in the way of oratory in 2008 and 2009 concerning the worst recession in immediate history: next to nothing.

The rest of the world is not much better. Political performances at what were once great political debating centers, for example, Brussels, Sofia, Washington DC, Ottawa, Copenhagen, Berlin, New Delhi, or Canberra, have descended into cant and unpersuasive repetition. And as for business speeches, there are very few worthy of the epithet "great." One must suppose that the most obvious reason for this is even if an MP, senator, government representative, or business executive had a tongue as silvery as Demosthenes', he or she may think that no matter what is said nothing will change. The worrying thing is that no government or other body anywhere shows much interest in trying to alter this perception. Also, few politicians or business executives consider it part of their responsibility to try to cultivate a charismatic speaking style. Perhaps that's because only a handful think that oratory has value. There will always be those whose minds are too prosaic to appreciate the lyricism of a great address. It is also true, of course, that politicians and executives tend to "save" their witty retorts, their smart sound bites, and their headline news. Why, they consider, should they expend their wittiest, cleverest, sharpest retorts on empty debating chambers or private meetings when they can keep them for blogs or comfortable chairs in the quiet and relative safety of a TV or radio studio, where a listening audience is guaranteed? Although even from a TV studio, while an audience may be guaranteed, viewers are not by any means guaranteed much in the way of great speaking or cogent ideas.

It's more than one smart line that makes a speech memorable—or great. It is a combination of things: behavior on (and off) the stage, setting, backdrop, props, set, environment, lighting, sound system, clothes, mood, techniques, body language, drama, moment in time—a tragedy, a celebration, a win, a loss, a personality—a single point to make, lives to save, sales to communicate to Sally Shoesmith. It's when the speaker, the moment, and the issues blend. It's what resonates brilliantly well with the audience. It's having something important to say—really important to you and to your audience, not just general guff.

Admire Good Writing

Speechwriters are important, of course. In the United States, Herbert Hoover was the last president not to use a professional writer; in the United Kingdom Winston Churchill was the last prime minister not to use one. Obviously, senior politicians are busy, and there is no expectation these days that a script or speech should be written by the speechmaker. However, the speechwriter has to be more than just good at writing; he or she has to really understand the speaker, the speaker's delivery style, and the speaker's stage presence. The writer also has to understand stagecraft and how the speaker will present, how the speaker will mouth words and phrases, how pauses will be used. The writer has to comprehend the power of oratory.

This is a skill and a half. Ted Sorensen, John F. Kennedy's policy adviser and wonderful speechwriter in chief (please read some of his work), created all of the great Kennedy speeches, lines from which are quoted each day in the media somewhere in the world. Sorensen was simply superb as a wordsmith, and he had in JFK a brilliant deliverer. It's the same with Obama, whose top wordsmith, Jon Favreau, totally understands the way that his boss thinks, speaks, and moves. He hears the intonation, the weft and weave of the stops and starts, the pauses, the intakes of breath, the verbal underlining, the wave of a hand, the pointing finger, the smile—even the walk up the steps to the stage or the approach to the lectern. Favreau is extraordinary, and each country has a number of writers like him, working in TV or advertising or for politicians and for business executives. But there are too few around.

Great writing and great delivery do exist. You have only to look at John McCain's concession speech to see a great example of great writing. The speech and its delivery were superb. Read it, or better still read it *and* listen to it. Had McCain given speeches like this during the whole campaign, well then the picture may have been very different or certainly closer. So, good writing, brilliant structure—such things matter as much as great delivery. But a brilliantly written, wonderfully structured speech is of no value if it's delivered badly. Your own personality, manner, and behavior also play a big part in how you'll be considered on a stage in front of any audience. Personality is important. This explains much of the public appeal of Bill Clinton. Clinton has that rare gift—a capacity to connect accurately and with an ability to make each person in a crowd feel as if he were talking directly to him or her. Clinton "gets" what an audience wants or needs. You simply cannot deliver a great speech unless you understand your audience. In 2000 at his final address to a Democratic convention as president, Clinton cited Harry Truman: "If you want to live like a Republican, you should vote for the Democrats." This showed that he understood precisely what the audience wanted and needed to hear; you could almost hear Republican strategists frowning in dismay, eager to get Clinton off the stage and bring Al Gore forward. But then Gore did step forward on the high stage and embarrassingly kissed his wife for an eon, which perhaps blew his chances. Remember, it's not always what you say when the spotlight is on you, it's also how you behave: What you do when waiting on the couch for the Q&A to begin or the conference to start, or when you're standing looking at your notes, or what you do that evening after the event's finished at dinner with colleagues. As you become known for your rhetoric and oratory, how you're seen to behave—always—is important. One reinforces a view of the other. It also shows that the whole establishment of what makes great speeches and great speakers is not just oratory alone but a heady mix.

Good Structure is Important

Every continent, every country has its great political orators of the past, but there are far fewer in evidence now. You can't look too closely at the business community for oratory either, because few examples exist. Many political and corporate speeches today make weak arguments and reference the lowest common denominator of culture, slang, and argument by bullying. Or they cram an hour full of PowerPoint and whizz the whole thing right over an audience's collective head. Or bore the poor delegate rigid. That's crazy because people in any land on earth want leadership, words of encouragement and praise, guidance, information, direction, and their hearts to sing. The young find this too: They like and want great words on issues that matter to them. A huge proportion of Obama's followers were under twenty. Why? Most, when questioned, said they liked his confidence, his idealism, and the way he spoke his words.

Oratory and rhetoric are the starting point, the bedrock of public speaking. To speak brilliantly in public involves practice, rehearsal, preparation, a deep love of words, reading, research, and knowledge (subject and general). Oratory is also about courage, emotion, standing (and standing up) for something, belief, and passion. This smorgasbord of "must haves" is as important when delivering a presidential address as it is when making a presentation to a small group of business colleagues just before the weekend. Yes, of course, there are degrees and levels of importance and there are economies of scale (one audience of ten thousand will have a bigger mix of attitudes than another of ten, but possibly not by much). In any speech and for any speaker, the ingredients don't really vary. And let's be very clear here—the defining scope of what comprises a great speaker is often surprising. It's a little like imagining quite wrongly what a radio announcer looks like. Some great speakers of history were, or are, short, tall, fat, thin, poorly educated, well educated, ill-mannered, well-mannered, murderous, evil, or golden in their goodness. All faced the challenge of "the speech" and speaking in public. Some relished the thought but knew that they had to work at it. Some were (and indeed surprisingly even today some famous people are), physically ill at the prospect. Few could stand up in front of an audience and find themselves to be natural orators with little preparation and no thought of what the audience needed or wanted.

So do we when we get a chance, really enjoy listening to great words structured to amuse, inform, and reach the mood of the moment? The world of entertainment shows us that yes, we do. And there's not a great difference in the setup between regular showmanship, entertainment, and speechmaking. While technology is responsible (in part) for changing our expectations for good public discourse, we can still find the occasional contemporary campaign and policy or business speech more than worthy of our attention. And we have to consider why. Is it easy to talk like a president? Do we want to? Well, from time to time, there is a need to stand on a stage, no matter how metaphorical or small, to present to or address a group of other people, no matter how few or how many. You can own the ingredients that are necessary to speak like a president. Not necessarily like Obama, but like you.

POINTS TO REMEMBER

- Performance is important no matter what the size of the audience. You have to work hard make the audience want to see and hear you again. Always, always be aware of your audience and what the people in it need or want to hear.
- If you're actually going to make a speech, and one presumes that you want to, then think about how to make it brilliantly.
- Orchestrate your actions: Consider beforehand everything that you do "onstage."
- You don't have to be a president (of anything) to speak like a president.
- Think about someone whose speeches you admire— anyone. Why do you like what this person says and how she or he says it? What can you learn?
- Learn from great speakers from history and some from today. Read famous speeches. Hear them if you can. Listen out for clever phraseology on the radio, on TV, on the bus.
- Good quality writing of any speech is so important. If you need help in writing your speeches, ask for it.
- Remember, it's not always what you say when the spotlight is on you that's important. It's also how you behave offstage or when you think you can't be seen.
- Know as much as you can about oratory and rhetoric: They are the bedrock of speechmaking.

Chapter Three
Tell Them a Story

"'Thou shalt not' is soon forgotten, but 'Once upon a time' lasts forever."
Philip Pullman (1946–)

Storytelling is important and it always has been. Storytelling is a way of amazing audiences, making a moral point, illustrating an issue, or explaining an otherwise complicated idea. All religions use storytelling as a way of showing right from wrong, good from evil, sadness from humor and so on. We all like stories. As small children we liked stories and now as adults we like them—on TV, in movies, plays, books, and speeches. Telling a story is an art and not everyone's good at it. You have to remember the salient points that illustrate what you want to say—your message—and you have to know the story inside out. You really don't want to stand there having forgotten a crucial part! Telling a story, a good story, is a way of grabbing your audience's interest, particularly if you know that the story or its message is relevant to the people in front of you. This comes back to knowing your audience, of course. And if you're going to start your speech by telling a story or a joke (they're often much the same thing), you have to be sure that the story is relevant and sound. This is crucial to winning an audience's trust. First impressions count for a lot. You have a small window at the beginning of your speech to "say" to people: "It's OK, I understand you and I can be amusing/ entertaining/witty/clever. You're going to have an interesting time in my care." Telling a good story, or explaining something using a narrative style, also allows an audience some breathing space.

People can (and need to) relax and enjoy your words, the humor, the pathos and the content.

Stories Can Make Your Speech Memorable

It is important to determine the main points you want to make in your speech and integrate stories that pertain to them. But avoid inserting random stories simply designed to make the speech more interesting. The audience will remember the anecdote instead of the true meaning of your address. Or people may not remember either. A story has to underline your message, not replace it. Experiment with the position of your anecdotes in the speech. Determine where they'll have the most impact and where they'll help your key points to be more memorable or interesting. Use them as links, introductions, or conclusions. A good story can act as an excellent bridge from one part of a speech to another. Match the story's tone to the mood of your speech. Use humor when it's appropriate or a touching story when you want to move your audience. To reiterate, be very careful that you know that the audience will appreciate the touching story or the humorous narrative!

Anything worthwhile is comprised of very large challenges. Public speakers have to face them, no matter how great anyone is at presenting a message or idea. The biggest challenge the speaker ultimately (constantly and unsurprisingly) faces is keeping his or her audiences interested in what they have to say. The greatest speakers—politicians, business people, brides' fathers, eulogy deliverers—all tell brilliant stories. Storytelling is one of the bases of great speechmaking. Not necessarily complicated or long, convoluted stories but, nonetheless, stories that make a strong point, stories that amuse, stories that reinforce a message, stories that sadden, stories that make us all consider something in a different light. Think about it—all cultures throughout the world have a strong tradition of storytelling, and stories have obviously been engaging audiences since the year one. We can all of us tell a story to a greater or lesser degree. You hear stories on the bus or train to work, stories on the radio, and stories in news items. Blogs are all about storytelling. You hear stories at coffee breaks and around water coolers. Newspapers tell stories and call their content stories. Jokes are mostly stories. Stories are what most of us tell on the phone. Stories give us insights. Some, but not enough, business leaders engage their people in strategy, vision, values, and change. They try to connect people and ideas through storytelling. Stories shape our dreams, and they allow us, in turn, to give a shape to our experiences. Stories are what we see and hear on TV screens, in cinemas, and at the theater. Theme parks are based on stories. Stories help children and adults learn, absorb facts, share information, and make ideas clear. We remember stories. Stories persuade and inspire. Stories, well told, have a far longer shelf life than the dry, abstract, one-way methods of corporate and political communications that clutter businesses and government communications and many business courses today. Stories can demonstrate what success or happiness looks and feels like. Stories can show us what it'll be like when we get to wherever the storyteller is persuading us to go. Stories can be used for good and, undeniably, for bad.

Stories Can Be Based On Anything

Borrow a story if you don't have one that illustrates your point or message. Draw from the experiences of your family and friends or reference a moment in a movie, book or famous historical speech. Do remember to give credit to the story's source before you tell it. It's a courtesy and it will normally appeal to the audience that you have credited the tale. Embellish your story, if necessary, but don't embellish it so much that the original point is lost. The most important thing is to practice telling the story often until your tone, pauses, voice, descriptions and timing are natural. Also, listen to famous public speakers to discover how they make their storytelling more effective.

In speechmaking, stories can be based on your personal experience. You may not think so, but you will have experienced and seen things that will make a great story. You can use versions of well-known stories or versions of other people's stories that you've read or heard. Really any story will do provided it's relevant and interesting. And that means bull's-eye relevant. Relevancy is very important, particularly given that an aim of any speech or presentation is to hold focus and interest. It's simply mind-boggling to hear time after time presentations in business and in politics where the relevancy is missing. Where has the focus gone, you muse before turning off the yawningly boring politician? Why is the politician boring? He or she is in an extraordinary sphere of life that necessitates that he or she should be interesting and have all of the qualities of a great speaker. In days gone by, politicians everywhere were expected to be better than reasonable orators.

Storytelling in Politics

In the modern age, great storytelling perhaps began an insurgence in politics during FDR's administration in America. He's the one famous for the following quote from his first inaugural address, given on March 4, 1933. You can understand the context of course: "The only thing we have to fear is fear itself...These dark days will be worth all they cost us if they teach us that our true destiny is not to be ministered unto but to minister to ourselves and to our fellow men." Roosevelt inspired people individually in one-to-one meetings, and he could do the same using the new mass medium of radio. He knew how to speak for different occasions, when to drop his voice or raise it, when to sound like everyone's favorite uncle or perhaps grandfather, and when to sound like a leader with spark, vitality, and direction. During the dark days of the Depression, he pioneered the "fireside chat"—the use of radio broadcasts to appeal to the American people simply and directly to gain support for his policies. In these broadcasts, FDR spoke to over sixty million Americans as if he were confiding openly and honestly to a single buddy in the privacy of the Oval Office. And he told stories.

After FDR, Americans expected a similar homely approach from all their presidents. Grand, eloquent speeches were considered a bit suspect, smacking of pretension and the lack of a common touch. Yet the reception and praise given to Barack Obama's speeches suggest that, despite the advent of TV, the Internet, and instant communications, there has been an untapped hunger for storytelling to inspire ordinary people and touch their ideals (although the ancient Greeks would have perhaps criticized Obama's speeches for sometimes emphasizing style over substance). Words still count and people like anecdotes, clever metaphors, and stories.

Storytelling is a Powerful Device

These days marketing (and much else) relies on storytelling. Managers tell stories to motivate their employees and spin doctors build a political story as if it were a real or true narrative. Stories used in politics are designed to bewitch or shock the listener or the reader. As a consequence of stories that we end up believing, we become immersed in a fictional world that filters our perceptions, prompts responses or feelings and frames our point of view. Sometimes the fictional worlds are accurate, but sometimes they are absolutely not. Frequently, we hear or read about stories that seem like reality where the reality reinforces a point or a set of figures. Using stories as examples of behavior are commonplace in business and politics. On the whole we are influenced by them. So, the orator's task has a built-in responsibility. You need to use stories with care. Casting cynicism aside, stories should be used to reinforce positives not to persuade people of something that is "true" but blatantly isn't. The spirit of storytelling in most speeches rests with an opportunity to clarify, entertain and reinforce.

There are stories used in politics and business which people want to hear because they make the listener feel better or more cheerful. That's fine as long as the purpose and intent are clear. Good stories don't just happen. A unified narrative isn't that easy and needs practice and work. The plot, characters, and descriptions mix to create a heady and satisfying whole. It was Aristotle who pointed out in his *Poetics* that a good story must have a beginning, middle and end. This isn't as silly or obvious as it may first sound. There are unbelievably large numbers of minor or mainstream corporate and political speeches that contain stories with only one or two of Aristotle's ingredients. A story without an ending, you will consider, isn't a story. That's absolutely correct, as it is when a "story" has no proper middle or end and sometimes no obvious or clear beginning. Just for the record, all stories or anecdotes need three key elements: a beginning, which sets the scene and introduces the plot or idea along with the main characters and the conflict or issue; a body, in which the conflict or issue builds to a climax or high point; followed by the conclusion, resolution of the conflict, or punch line.

As you become more adept at storytelling, you can be bolder and use stories that require various character voices, gestures (keep them big) and exaggeration of scenes or details. And, as your confidence grows, you can also introduce unusual or unexpected twists in the narration of your tale. You can also add throw-away lines or asides and that has particular value if you know your audience very well indeed. It creates a warmth and familiarity. Your listeners will feel that the asides are specifically for them and they will like that. One warning shot across your bow: once you've finished the story, joke, or anecdote, stop and move on. Don't mutter and ramble. Don't apologize for the story if it hasn't "worked." Don't explain the story or feel obliged to tie up any loose ends. Don't be embarrassed. Applause, by the by, is no great measure of a story well told. Sometimes an audience will show its appreciation, sometimes an audience won't. But the latter doesn't mean that people aren't considering what you've said or what point you've made. The most important thing is that you have fun. If you do, then it's more likely that the audience will too.

Stories are kept alive, as are jokes, through re-telling. In that process they become richer and usually (but not always) better; some stories benefit from little adjectival expansion, others benefit from more detail. There is no hard and fast rule here, but you will know what works after a while. That sounds as if you should submit yourself to trial by fire, but each speech and each story will be different. The best rule of thumb is to keep a story short, not so short that it's stripped and is now devoid of color or a focus for imagination, but short enough so that the point is made and you can move on with the rest of what you have to say. What you say and how you tell your story does much depend on the composition of your audience. Some may like their senses to be stimulated so that they can "visualize" the detail and see that the vivid word pictures can come alive. A good story will help an audience to sympathize with characters where you want them to sympathize or to laugh at or with characters where you so direct.

Learn From the Greats

Charles Dickens is rightly regarded as one of the world's truly great novelists. He was also famous for reading his own books aloud to huge acclaim and for lecturing on the social mores of Victorian England. His books had a particular flow and rhythm, punctuated by one shock or cliffhanger after another with the public avidly looking forward to the next installment with bated breath. On the lecture circuit his presentation technique was to keep his audiences focused, and his skill was to create anticipation. He was the consummate storyteller. In his stories, the characters were often exaggerations of good and bad. This is interesting, since exaggerating characters (not the same as telling untruths of course), is often a good way of attracting an audience's attention and keeping that attention focused. Making characters larger than life is as enjoyable for an adult listener as it is for a child. Dickens was like an actor in the way that he told his tales or lectured on poverty or child cruelty. His voice would rise to a terrifying crescendo and fall, sometimes to a whisper. He would imitate accents and take the part of characters with gusto in order to make a point. Any speech of his was theatrical and dramatic. Audiences were spellbound. He was a true storyteller to whom people would listen for hours, often in tears at his narration of some aspect of London's slums or roaring with laughter at his description of a factory owner or politician. However, please don't forget that a speech is not always solely about entertaining your audience (although that can be important) as it is an opportunity to move your strategy, message, or plan forward, to reinforce argument, and to persuade your listeners that your views are worthwhile.

Most of Dickens's public speeches and readings from his work were packed, both in the United Kingdom and the United States. On his last public presentation on March 15, 1870, at St James's Hall in London, and amid repeated acclamations, with hats and handkerchiefs apparently waving in every part of the hall, Dickens retired, withdrawing one of the greatest intellectual treats the public ever enjoyed. Whether or not people have paid money to see you, they have paid with their time. You, the speaker, owe them a certain respect. Therefore, speakers should always put on their best performance and effort. That evening, Dickens read with as much spirit and energy as he ever did. His readings from *Oliver Twist*, particularly the emotionally charged Nancy and Bill Sikes scenes, were received with rapturous applause. But then, he always made a point of preparing properly and of understanding what his audiences liked, what made them laugh, gasp in horror, or cry. His voice, to the end, retained its distinctive clarity, excellent projection, and great expression. Each character in each passage came alive by a simple transition of tone, a pause, or a specific stressed word, an inflection here and a hoarse whisper there. People could all but see the vividly painted characters before them. It is not a dissimilar picture from watching one of the world's great theater actors on stage, people like Peter O'Toole, John Gielgud, Ian McKellen, Derek Jacobi, Anthony Sher, or Kevin Spacey and so on. When you see a great actor "tell" a play's story, you know you have experienced something great.

If you consider some of the best ever speeches, the ingredients are plain to see. They are delivered by great presenters of information who make us, the audience, believe that what they have to say is true. What we all look for in many speeches is the telling of a good story. And for you as someone who might want to be a great speaker, you have to know good stories to gain an understanding of what works, to get a grip on what makes a good beginning, middle, and end, what excites, amuses, horrifies, pleases, gladdens. Reading good stories is important if you're going to *tell* good stories. To be a great speechmaker, you do need to read extensively not least to understand what comprises a great story but also to learn about the use of language.

Select Appropriate Stories

If you don't have a story that illustrates your point or message, borrow one. Draw from the experiences of your family and friends or reference a moment in a movie, book or famous historical speech. Embellish your story, if necessary, but don't embellish it so much that the original point is lost. The most important thing is to practice telling the story often until your tone, pauses, voice, descriptions and timing are natural. Also, listen to famous public speakers to discover how they make their storytelling more effective.

Select stories that are a good match for your storytelling skills. Yes, we all have some, but they need to be honed. Think about how you can set the scene, especially as it contributes to the mood and spirit of the story. Bring the characters to life. Lose your inhibitions. Think character. Characterization is very important. Use dialogue to make it seem as though the characters are right there with you and your audience. If that means doing funny voices, fine.

If you don't want to do that, that's fine too. Make the way of telling a story your own. Accentuate the plot so that your audience can experience the highs and lows of the story, the sad and the funny, the silly and the serious, the pause for effect, the clever phrase. Present the story so the listeners can follow you through your sequence of events. Good storytelling is powerful and can motivate people as well as entertain them. Your influence as a storyteller is beyond words, but your choice of words, body language, facial expressions, and interpretations (and, don't forget, relevance) are the things that can make a story work.

But be aware of your audience, and don't push the audience's patience. Keep the story short. Practice your pacing. Practice too how you will put together your words, what movement you might use, how you'll use particular phrases, and character traits. Think about descriptions of people and places which in themselves can be entertaining. Think about facial expressions. Of course, be wary of allowing your facial expressions to do too much "work." Not everyone may be able to see you in detail, particularly if you are in a large auditorium or the audience is big in number. Some events will have cameras picking up your every wince, smile or grimace and projecting your head and shoulders on large screens. Be aware that this is the case and make it your business to find out if this is so well before the speaking engagement.

Storytelling is one of the best tools a public speaker can use to relate to an audience. Through storytelling the members of an audience should be able to identify with the story and also with you. They may have had the same experience or at least they will have witnessed a similar "event" in real life. If you throw a story into your presentation that has no bearing on your subject matter, it will only serve to confuse your listeners and it is very hard to recover "trust" or interest from an audience once it's lost. Telling stories is a good way to communicate a unique or common experience. Storytelling creates an intimacy and, if you add a story or stories to your speech, you will be connecting to your audience members on a very intimate level, thus breaking down barriers and creating a better conduit between you and them.

Storytelling Can Make a Speaker's Life Easier

Funnily enough it's not just people who make speeches who get nervous. Some people have anxiety about having to listen to a speech, particularly if the audience numbers are small. There's less to hide behind. People aren't always sure how to behave or what might be expected of them. It's like going to the theater when you discover to your (and certainly to my) dismay that sitting in the front row is likely to mean that you will be expected to be involved with the stage action. If you add a story to your speech, any uncomfortable listeners will probably relax, understanding that they can simply allow themselves to absorb what you're saying without worrying if they are likely to be called on to do something. Don't disappoint them!

Stories can be used to make an audience reconsider their own thoughts or beliefs. And, actually, telling stories can be fun for *you*, particularly if you know the story inside out. You will enjoy the process and you can put down your notes.

You as a Source

As indicated, the best source of stories that you can tell to your audience is your personal experience. This will help you to get closer to your audience since your personal experience will show an audience that you've also been in situations and have had experiences with which listeners might identify. Tell a story about yourself. Even if it's not incredibly personal, state it as though it's a secret you're sharing with your listeners. As a result, they'll be more likely to feel like you've been open with them. Your first port of call in finding material for your speeches and presentations must be your own life. You are sure to find amusing anecdotes and life-defining moments. It is these stories and experiences that make you unique and, what's more, no one can tell these stories like you can. Even if others may later tell your life story, only you can tell it in the first person. At first, it may be a little disconcerting to expose yourself and your life in this way. You may feel hesitant at revealing your foibles but it's these which help you to build a connection with your audience. Your listeners are looking for a guiding light, for inspiration. They will receive your message more readily if it is seen to have come from someone who isn't perfect. This gives them hope that if you can overcome your limitations then they too can overcome their limiting and negative beliefs and achieve whatever it is you're speaking about.

Wherever you source a story, know it like the back of your hand. And bear in mind that you should tell your stories that have a theme related to your speech. Make sure that your stories will help clarify or support your theme. It makes sense to choose a story or tale that has as much universal appeal as possible. Unless you know unequivocally that your audience is specialist and will understand a joke or story about a specific topic, be wary. Similarly, don't try and memorize the words of the story, because you'll just set yourself up for confusion and what you say won't sound particularly natural. You need to tell a story in a way that the listener will think is as fresh as it was the first time you ever told it.

So that you don't have to spend time scouring newspapers and the like, you can sign up to a service such as Google Alerts. Then you'll be notified of news stories that relate to your subject matter or to you. You just need to select your key words and choose how often you wish to receive alerts. You will then have an automatic way to keep abreast of the latest news stories on topics of your interest. And interest is key to the composition of your speeches.

POINTS TO REMEMBER

- Storytelling is a way of amazing audiences, making a moral point, illustrating an issue, and explaining an otherwise complicated idea.
- All great speakers use stories. One of the main differences in the last American general election was Barack Obama's ability to persuade. Another big difference was Obama's knack for storytelling and how he was able to maintain a compelling narrative.
- There are many business presentations through which people sit but by the end they couldn't tell anyone much about the content or message. It's not that the speaker was necessarily bad: It's just that nothing that they said caught their audience's imagination and so nothing stuck. This is where stories come in—people remember stories.
- Stories empower the speaker. They can be used to create a particular environment or atmosphere. They can reinforce and clarify the message or messages within a speech.
- There are a variety of types of stories. Stories about you can be used to gain an audience's trust by explaining something of your background and your expertise or by the fact that you're the same as the people in the audience and share their concerns, fears, worries. Or you can use a story to explain your agenda. Stories can be used to paint a vision of the future that the audience can see and of which they may subsequently want to be a part. Stories can help share the good things that can happen when an audience has shared values.
- Stories can demonstrate what success (or failure) looks like.
- Like any aspect of speechmaking, you have to practice storytelling.
- Select stories that are a match for your storytelling skills. As you improve or get better, then be more adventurous.

Chapter Four
Now, Go to the Movies

"Every time I go to a movie, it's magic, no matter what the movie's about."
Steven Spielberg (1946–)

Widening the scope for emulating great speeches and great situations from which to learn, we should look hard at the world of entertainment as well as the world of stories and storytelling. Sometimes these things are complementary. As with good stories, great movies or plays make us want more—either from the same writer, director, or actor. Recall your favorite moments in the theater or movies. How did they make you feel? Why are they inspirational, interesting, sad, funny, moving, powerful, exciting, wish-you-were-there good? All of those scenes and lines that you like are probably scenes and lines that many others like too. Use them to populate speeches. Get people to say to themselves, "Oh yes, I remember that moment. I get that."

There Are Many Movies From Which You Can Source Ideas

Savor a scene from *Scent of a Woman* (1992), in which Al Pacino, plays a blind, depressed, and disillusioned retired army colonel, Frank Slade. At one point he speaks up on behalf of his part-time minder and companion, Charlie Sims, an inexperienced and naïve but essentially good-hearted seventeen-year-old. Charlie is a privately educated schoolboy on a scholarship and is hated by the thicker, richer few (led by the nastiest boy, called George, played by a reasonably youthful Philip Seymour Hoffman) who are jealous of Charlie's good nature and appeal. The scene is one where the school's principal, Mr Trask, is prepared to lead an unpleasant cover-up, part of which involves dismissing Charlie in the erroneous belief, based on hearsay, that the boy has let down the school and his peers. Trask takes the side of the bully boys, maybe because he's also a bully and because the parents of the school bullies give a great deal of money to the school. All seems lost for Charlie's future, when suddenly the auditorium's double doors burst open and the magnificent tap-tap of blind Colonel Slade's stick is all that is heard as he makes his way to the stage. Having insisted on wanting to say something, he makes a speech that is utterly superb and spellbinding. Here's a taste: "Here's Charlie facing the fire; and there's George hidin' in big daddy's pocket. And what are you doin'? You're gonna reward George and destroy Charlie...I don't know who went to this place, William Howard Taft, William Jennings Bryan, William Tell—whoever. Their spirit is dead—if they ever had one—it's gone...If you think you're preparing these minnows for manhood, you better think again. Because I say you are killing the very spirit this institution proclaims it instills!...The only class in this act is sittin' next to me." This is not, by any stretch, a business or political speech (although if some of both had an element of this fire, then perhaps we'd get a more committed electorate or workforce around the world), but you can surely see how the technique, the words, and the buildup could work for you. Not all of the time of course and not always with the anger or vocabulary that's contained in this scene, but the power of a speech can work for you. Study these things. You don't have to copy Al Pacino and it'd be crazy to try, but you can learn from films, for example, how speeches are delivered. You can also use scenes like this to reinforce a point that you're making.

Take a look too at the closing scenes of *Lord of the Rings—Return of the King* (2003). Whatever you may think of the three movies, there is a scene in the last one that melts hearts and it's so easy to use the scene to make a point. Aragorn is crowned king, heralding the new age of peace, and is reunited with Arwen. When Aragorn sees the hobbits bow before him in recognition of his royalty, he stops them and says, "You bow to no one," and it is he who then kneels before them in honor of their sacrifice, following which the multitude that is Minas Tirith bows and kneels to the hobbits. Wonderful stuff! You don't have to be a J. R. R. Tolkien fan or a lover of Peter Jackson's work to see how the moment can be powerful. And powerful moments have a big part to play in speeches. The *Lord of the Rings—Return of the King* scene is not a speech, but it's a picture, and you can create that kind of picture as a story in any speech of yours. You don't need to be a hobbit or a king, but you can use a version of the phrase "you bow to no one" and the relevant scene in your own context and to your own advantage. Try it.

Then there are the films where the alpha leader rallies thousands of scared and uncertain warriors to bring out their fighting spirit before a huge battle. In *Braveheart* (1995), Mel Gibson's William Wallace boasts that their (the Scots') enemies "can take their lives, but they can never take their freedom." Similarly, in *Gladiator* (2000), General Maximus Decimus Meridius (Russell Crowe) gives his opening battle address to the Roman cavalry and readies his lieutenants prior to the first battle of the movie with the Germans. He tells them, "Fratres! Three weeks from now I will be harvesting my crops. Imagine where you will be and it will be so. Hold the line! Stay with me! If you find yourself alone, riding in green fields with the sun on your face, do not be troubled, for you are in Elysium and you're already dead! Brothers, what we do in life echoes in eternity." Again, don't think for one single minute that there is necessary merit in daubing your body in blue woad or dressing up as a gladiator or indeed in quoting such lines verbatim, unless the phrase really works to make a point (and please don't discount the power of doing that—provided the result doesn't sound trite). The point is that you can use powerful filmic devices to reinforce the thrust of your argument: "As so and so says when the battle was nearly lost..." or "Let me describe a scene to you..."

Glengarry Glen Ross (1992), based on the David Mamet play of the same name, is another movie filled with heavy-hitting speech talent. It's the story of salesmen who would do anything to get leads and make sales, only they don't do very much of either. This is a character-driven piece with pre-fame Kevin Spacey as a creepy office boss and Al Pacino, Jack Lemmon, Ed Harris, and Alan Arkin as account executives who seem to be past their prime and in much need of a motivational lift, only they don't want one. Throughout the film there are speeches that plead, exhort, castigate, and delight in the use of language and persuasion. Again, nobody is suggesting that you must use the phrases and exact words of a movie, but it may be useful to quote the scenes or a few apposite lines to illustrate your point. Stick to movies or TV programs that are popular or that you know most in your audience will have seen.

George C. Scott played General George S. Patton in the film *Patton* (1970). Scott won an Oscar for his portrayal of the famous soldier, and his strong performance was in itself much like an artillery bombardment. At the beginning of the movie, with the backdrop of a giant American flag, Patton climbed a stage to give a six-and-a-half minute speech to soldiers you never see. Actually, the soldiers are us, the audience. The speech was part of a real speech Patton had given many times to rousing choruses of cheers from the troops. Another example is the "You can't handle the truth" speech given by Jack Nicholson to Tom Cruise in *A Few Good Men* (1992). And then there's the wonderful courtroom scene where Gregory Peck defends Tom in *To Kill a Mockingbird* (1962). Then there's the astonishing "I'm mad as hell" speech given by Peter Finch in the movie *Network* (1976). The point is that anyone can be a speechmaker. And a great one too. *You* pick your words, *you* control what you say and how you say it. Models from movies are just as valid as those from presidents, politics, and business.

The Theater Is a Good Source of Ideas Too

Movies aren't the only source of material and ideas, of course. The theater is a great larder from which ideas can be garnered. Go to the theater. Watch how professional actors deliver words. The St. Crispin's Day speech given by King Henry V prior to the Battle of Agincourt in William Shakespeare's *Henry V* is well known and has been used to whip up patriotism and the value of leadership. You may not wish to deliver Shakespeare at a Sally Shoesmith sales meeting on a wet Wednesday afternoon, but on the other hand you just might if it was relevant, and indeed Ms Shoesmith might be impressed. Certainly, there are things you can learn from Shakespeare to make what you say superb. Also, his stories (*Romeo and Juliet*, *Richard III*, *Julius Caesar*, *Hamlet* and the rest) all work as points of reference. That's the beauty of Shakespeare. Don't forget that it's your job to make people want to hear what you have to say, so raid as many sources as possible to make your message clear. Make people in your audiences wait upon your every word, every pause, and every action.

If you really want be a great speaker, you have to watch and listen and read great speeches. You're not trying to be someone else—you're being you—but you're adding weight to what you say and how you deliver it. That's what great speakers have done throughout history. Sourcing material and ideas from the world of entertainment is beneficial if you want to make short, sharp points relating to the "here and now." Only use material with which you feel totally comfortable and which suits your personality. Don't use material that you don't understand and don't try and be too clever—your audiences may not understand and your goose will be cooked. The quotes don't all have to be filmic or literary. Popular culture and the culture of soaps work as well. Some quotations from the good and great emanating from the world of rock and roll might work for you too. Quote them if they're relevant. Here are a few alleged ones that can work. Billy Joel, singer and songwriter: "Videos destroyed the vitality of rock and roll. Before that music said, 'Listen to me.' Now it says, 'Look at me.'" And Elvis Presley said: "I don't know anything about music. In my line you don't have to." Jimmy Page of Led Zeppelin apparently said: "I always thought the good thing about the guitar was that they didn't teach it in school." Keith Richards of the Rolling Stones: "Everyone talks about rock these days; the problem is they forget about the roll." And Dave Gilmour of Pink Floyd: "Where would rock and roll be without feedback?" Dennis Hopper: "Just because it happened to you, doesn't mean it's interesting."

Search for Material to Suit Your Argument

Search for material to suit *your* argument. Read, watch, and observe. Consider quotes and phrases, and consider how actors deliver speeches on the stage and on the screen, how they move and how they say what they say. Absorb it all. Then think about how to make your points. How can you make your proposition work? What will support it? What would make it come alive? What can you add to illustrate what you want to say? Think what it'll be like to be a great speaker. Be a great speaker.

POINTS TO REMEMBER

- There are many movies to watch in all languages from which you can get some good ideas about speeches and speechmakers.
- In no particular order here are a few that are worthy of a look and listen: *Adam's Rib* (1949), where Doris Attinger testifies about her husband's murder, or where Amanda Bonner delivers closing arguments; *Air Force One* (1998), where President Marshall makes an antiterrorism speech; *All the King's Men* (1949), where newly elected governor

Willie Stark addresses the people; *A Man for All Seasons* (1966), where Sir Thomas More makes his quiet but firm final speech to the court; *An Ideal Husband* (1999), where Sir Robert Chiltern addresses the House of Commons; *Chariots of Fire* (1981), where Eric Liddell speaks at the Scotland-versus-Ireland races, and where, on another occasion, the master of Caius, a Cambridge college, addresses the students; *Elizabeth* (1998), where the Queen of England addresses rival clergy on the topic of a unified church; *Field of Dreams* (1989), where the "If you build it, he will come" whisper will guarantee to make some of you cry shamelessly; *Gandhi* (1982), where Gandhi addresses the Indian National Congress; *Gods and Generals* (2003), where General Robert E. Lee accepts the Army of Virginia command, and also where Colonel Joshua Chamberlain tells of Caesar's crossing of the Rubicon; *Good Night and Good Luck* (2005), where Edward Murrow (in real life a brilliant orator—his writings are a must-read) addresses the Radio and TV News Directors Association and Foundation; *Inherit the Wind* (1960), where Colonel Drummond interrogates Matthew Brady on the scientific truth of the Bible; *Judgment at Nuremberg* (1961), where Judge Haywood delivers the court's decision; *MacArthur* (1977), where General Douglas MacArthur addresses West Point, and, by the way, this is in reality an outstandingly crafted speech as well as one superbly delivered both in the film and in real life; *Mr Smith Goes to Washington* (1939), where Senator Smith famously introduces the National Boys Camp bill; *Mrs Miniver* (1942), where the vicar gives a wonderfully moving sermon on the war; *Quiz Show* (1994), where Charles Van Doren testifies before the House Committee on Interstate and Foreign Commerce;

Remember the Titans (2000), where coach Herman Boone makes "his" Gettysburg speech; *Schindler's List* (1993), where Oskar Schindler delivers his farewell address to the Jewish factory workers who have worked for him to escape the death camps; *The Browning Version* (1951), where Mr Crocker-Harris declares his failure as a teacher; *Goodbye Mr Chips* (the 1969 version), where Peter O'Toole as Mr Chips addresses the whole school, thanking the boys and masters for their support—another great tearjerker; *There Will Be Blood* (2007), where Daniel Plainview speaks to the arguing landowners; *To Kill a Mockingbird* (1962), where Atticus Finch closes the argument at the Robinson Trial. These are but a few of many terrific movies from which you might pick a line or two or a scene to reinforce what you are saying. You may of course like none of them and that's fine too. Create your own list.

- There are also of course movies in languages other than English where we can learn from powerful or emotional speeches: *Cinema Paradiso* (Italian, 1988)—a heart-warming romantic comedy in which a young boy in a Sicilian village grows up under the influence of the town's film projectionist and later becomes a movie director in Rome; *Jean de Florette* and *Manon of the Spring* (French, 1986)—two movies, released together, about a greedy plot to deprive a man of his land, inherited from his mother, in rural Provence, and his daughter's determination to seek revenge years later; *City of God* (Brazilian, 2002)—a strong and not-for-the-faint-hearted movie depicting the street violence of Brazil's worst slum, built for the homeless and from which the ironic title derives; *Kolya* (Czech, 1996)—an Oscar-winning film about an aging cellist who marries to help a Russian woman emigrate and ends up with a great stepson; *Salaam Bombay!* (Indian, 1988)—a movie about Bombay's street children. And so on. Again, you'll want to research your own list and of course if you refer to a film or play, it does help if you've seen it!

- Sources of scenes and lines can come from mainstream TV, movies, theater and songs.

Chapter Five
Leadership

"If your actions inspire others to dream more, learn more, do more and become more, you are a leader."
John Quincy Adams (1767–1848)

In the delivery of speeches that embody leadership, consider building three-part, or triangular, phrases. We find these in the advertising of exceptionally successful firms such as Nike: "Just do it." We find them too in persuasive communications such as Obama's encouragement to a nation concerned about change: "Yes we can!" General MacArthur's brilliant speech celebrating West Point's motto and his own person credo, "Duty, Honor, Country," is another example. Read these words from the May 12, 1962 MacArthur speech (aloud if you want) and see how they deliver great power. They are also extraordinarily moving: "My days of old have vanished, tone and tint. They have gone glimmering through the dreams of things that were. Their memory is one of wondrous beauty, watered by tears, and coaxed and caressed by the smiles of yesterday. I listen vainly, but with thirsty ears, for the witching melody of faint bugles blowing reveille, of far drums beating the long roll. In my dreams I hear again the crash of guns, the rattle of musketry, the strange, mournful mutter of the battlefield. But in the evening of my memory, always I come back to West Point. Always there echoes and re-echoes: Duty, Honor, Country."

Look For Good, Supportive Statements Concerning Leadership

Take your pick of great statements about leadership. There are many, and they are easy to use in a speech and to support your proposition and argument. Sometimes they are too easy to use, and there's little worse than listening to a speech that is comprised mostly of others' words. Dull and boring. Each quotation on its own doesn't necessarily cut the mustard if used in isolation, but a good, carefully chosen, apposite quote does add value—particularly on leadership. There are many quotations on the subject of leadership. For example, Theodore Roosevelt said, "The best executive is the one who has sense enough to pick good men to do what he wants done and self-restraint to keep from meddling with them while they do it." Isaac Newton had this to say on leadership, "If I have seen farther than others, it is because I was standing on the shoulder of giants." And Winston Churchill said, "The price of greatness is responsibility." Whether you're speaking to Sally Shoesmith's sales team, a management group, two thousand employees or a TV audience of millions, consider that your speech will come from a leader. That's you. You don't have to lead a country to be regarded as a leader. Great speaking and great oratorical skills lead to leadership. You should embrace that.

Inspiring language is simple and clear. One of Churchill's strongest assets was oratory. As a young army officer stationed in India in 1897, he wrote that: "Of all the talents bestowed upon men, none is so precious as the gift of oratory." His speeches of 1940 became legendary, not only for their magnetism but, more importantly, for their simplicity, clever use of words and dynamic effect on public morale. To counter both the disastrous retreat from France and to put to rest any notion that Britain might capitulate, Churchill delivered one of his many patriotic speeches to Parliament on June 18 that was also broadcast by the BBC. He made no effort to hide under any carpet the extent of the dire situation Britain faced. Of

Hitler he said, "If we can stand up to him, all Europe may be free... But if we fail, then the whole world, including the United States, will sink into the abyss of a new Dark Age...Let us therefore brace ourselves to our duties and so bear ourselves that, if the British Empire and Commonwealth last for a thousand years, men will say, 'This was their finest hour.'" It doesn't mean of course that your speeches should contain similar phrases. One hopes, for instance, that you're not a prime minister in the midst of a world war. And it's important to note that language changes, and a speech that worked in 1940 is unlikely to work in the same way now. But the ingredients and the craft don't much change. The point here is that clever and pointed language can engender in your audience both emotion and, importantly, belief.

Rise to the Challenge of Leadership

Just as Churchill faced overwhelming odds against success, Barack Obama has faced and is facing challenges to overcome a crisis unprecedented since the Great Depression. The West shares far more than merely an imploded economy, including two major and expensive military conflicts that have lasted longer than World War II, an increasingly desperate situation in the Middle East, and education and health systems in jeopardy, to name just a few. In the case of the United States, Obama must rally a government in a dangerously unstable post-9/11 world in which the prestige of America has sunk to a low point. Britain and some of its European cousins, Greece, for example, fare little better. China is growing, as is India, and the emerging markets generally are pushing the West into a secondary position. Against this backdrop, what Obama and (some) other leaders have are oratorical skills comparable to Churchill's. What all nations (and collectives like the UN) need is a solid dose of inspiration to help guide people through hard times. People do want guidance, they want hope, and they want to make sense of the muddled messages they've been getting about global warming, religion, demographics, oil, water, wars, and finance. On ABC's *This Week* on January 11, 2009, Obama showed that he fully understands the power of oratory when he remarked that one of his roles as president is to "capture the moment" as a means of inspiring confidence. No less is this true for you—to capture the moment and inspire confidence.

In the end, inspired leadership counts for as much as, if not more than, clever political and economic decisions. The example set by Churchill is that there is absolutely no substitute for thoughtful and forceful oratory in a crisis or for vision and the power of reflection. The properly communicated promise that adversity can be overcome is a vital first step. Churchill offered hope for survival when there was nothing else, which makes the example he set as relevant today as it was seventy years ago.

Oratory is a Weapon

Oratory is the oldest of political weapons, and although its use has waned, its power never has. So it's strange indeed that more politicians and business executives don't take sufficient notice of the great weapon that is oratory. Think back to some key moments in speeches and history. When radio was king, a new president's powerful voice cut through the pessimism of the Great Depression: "So let me assert my firm belief that the only thing we have to fear... is fear itself." In the age of television, the youngest elected president spoke to his nation's and then other nations' aspirations: "I believe that this nation should commit itself to achieving the goal, before this decade is out, of landing a man on the moon and returning him safely to the Earth." A quarter of a century later, the oldest elected president acknowledged a country's grief: "We will never forget the last time we saw them, as they slipped the surly bonds of Earth to touch the face of God." And today, in a time of podcasts and Facebook, when rolling media assaults us in one-liners and clever headlines, is it really possible that the oldest of political and persuasive tools—the spoken word—is still one of the most powerful?

How else did a little-known state senator become a national phenomenon? With a single speech at a Democratic convention: "We worship an awesome God in the blue states and we have gay friends in the red states," Obama said, in his plea for unity. And it's not just in America that oratory plays its part. In Australia, Canada, China, Nigeria—in most countries—there are exemplary examples of oratory, some of it live, some of it via TV or the Internet or radio. In places where education is generally lacking, oratory is regarded highly. The small villages, regional meetings, and national gatherings in parts of Southeast Asia and Africa are full of oratory and storytelling, where the verve of the "point" is acknowledged and praised.

Leadership necessitates oratory. Not just on a presidential stage, but in the advertising agency office, when Sally Shoesmith has to show the latest sales figures to a group of junior executives. Can oratory count then? Oh, yes. Be the leader. Think like a leader. Act the part. Ronald Reagan was once asked, "How can you be an actor and be President?" And he thought about it and said, "I don't know how you can be President without being an actor." Sometimes, the right words of leadership change history. Consider what happened in March 1965, after civil rights demonstrators were met with violence by local officials in Selma, Alabama. President Lyndon B. Johnson spoke to a nationally televised joint session of Congress, urging lawmakers to pass the Voting Rights Act: "There must be no delay or no hesitation or no compromise with our purpose," he said. You can do that in your own way. Make the moment and the issues join together. "Really," said Johnson, "it's all of us who must overcome the crippling legacy of discrimination. And we shall overcome." And this came from a Southerner appropriating the anthem of the civil rights movement! What Johnson said resonated with the people, as he knew it would—not cynically, but because it helped him lead.

The golden rule of leading through oratory (if there really is one) is to say something important, and the silver rule is to make the audience understand that whatever you are saying *is* important. The bronze rule is to attach yourself or your topic to a moment of consequence to which you're responding—the conference, the event, Ms Shoesmith's sales meeting. It's this last that will actually get you noticed. And the topic can be anything: an unhappy workforce, a loss of a piece of business, a lost pitch, a won pitch, a retirement, a new recruit, a wedding, a hustings, a eulogy, a state of the nation.

Don't Fear Your Ability to Lead

The trouble is that many people believe that they can't lead. Many people say that they can't deliver an excellent speech. That probably isn't true at all. The fear of speaking in public (stage fright really) is called glossophobia, and it's very, very common. Get over the fright and you're on the way to the delivery of excellence. The main cause for fear is the lack of preparation. So prepare. Consider your main argument and your main points justifying that main argument. Don't get sidetracked. Consider your vocabulary, your voice register, and your choice of words. Make notes. Consider humor, gestures, where you will stand, and how you will stand. Consider how you will develop a relationship with the audience. The key to all of these things (including leadership of course) is character. Yours. A leader has to show his or her audience that the future is a shared one where everyone has a part to play to achieve whatever goals are being projected. Even if you're pitching to a potential client, this is so. Talk about a joint future. Even if you're presenting sales figures to your boss, Jack Shallowpockets, explain that the strategy is a joint one, not just your responsibility. Having established that the leader and the led are part of each other's future, you have to arrive at a shared and binding commitment in the face of, say, uncertainty or overwhelming odds, a tough economic climate, or whatever the issue. You get the picture.

We Warm to Great Leadership

It is of course human nature to warm to somebody with whom we can relate. A leader must convince an audience that the people in it have, at some stage, experienced the same confusions and contradictions as has he or she. And a leader must show a scenario that is attainable. A leader must include a vision of the future based on knowledge and experience of the past. Of course, to do much of this it's important to know yourself and be able to identify your personal values that will benefit you in leading people in a certain direction. Knowing your own values (not as trite as this may sound, by the way) helps you to weave your convictions into what you are trying to say and lets others know who you are and for what you stand. Self-knowledge is paramount. The great preacher-speakers of the nineteenth century and indeed some of the great politicians understood this well. Those who got it wrong were often unmasked as fakes. Audiences can by and large sense dishonesty even if the speaker is saying something that the listeners want to hear. Another factor altogether, unfortunately, is that they may choose to ignore the dishonesty.

The key to an effective leadership speech is structure. You must connect with your listeners by telling them where you've been (what you've done, say, to solve a problem), where you are (what you're doing now to sort it out), and where you're going (how the matter will be concluded). Relating to them directly will give people a sense that things are moving forward and that they can (really) contribute to the new future that you describe, even if it's "just" better sales figures next month. In the opening of your speech, you must prepare your audience to listen with open minds. You must acknowledge possible (and specific) opposition to your views. That's important—it removes the rug from under the feet of your gainsayers. If you can tell your listeners about the opposite angles to your argument, then few in the audience can say that you are being unreasonable. Similarly, if people believe that you are addressing their own very personal concerns, then you're on to a winner as well.

Franklin D. Roosevelt's fireside speech after Pearl Harbor (December 7, 1941) is a great example of rhetoric and leadership. And of addressing individual concerns. Radio was relatively new then, but the majority of Americans had access to one in cars and in homes as well as diners and restaurants. People enjoyed the natural manner in which the president spoke, as if to the listener personally. This is a great skill. If people in your audiences believe that you are speaking directly to them, you have almost won your cause. The day after his Pearl Harbor speech to Congress, FDR chose a fireside address to ready America for the unfathomable (and possibly terrifying) challenges ahead. In the middle of the speech, he stopped himself and said, "I was about to add that ahead there lies sacrifice for all of us. But it is not correct to use that word. The United States does not consider it a sacrifice to do all one can, to give one's best to our nation, when the nation is fighting for its existence." This was extraordinary and is still a technique used by many great orators. Stop yourself in mid flow, appear human and caring (because you are both), consider an issue as you stand there on stage, and then be very honest about your real concern. You have to know that your timing will work, and it's always a calculated risk. But then much of standing on any stage is a calculated risk. In this instance, FDR's honest assessment of the difficulties and forthright appeals to patriotism helped to inspire Americans to serve their country.

Bring Your Audience Behind Your Cause

On September 12, 1962, John F. Kennedy led America to a national commitment to land on the moon by the end of the decade, helping to transform the American economy. Consider that you might use the same device in your speeches—bringing your audience behind a cause. You don't have to say that they must do something, but say that we will do something. Kennedy didn't cover up the difficulties ahead: "We choose to go to the moon in this decade and do the other things, not because they are easy, but because they are hard." Leadership is important in any speech, which, if you think about it, is obvious. But leadership in a great speech is dynamite, something of course that Hitler, Mussolini, Saddam Hussein, the Iranian leadership, and others clearly realized. In more common scenarios, directors, senior managers, investors and voters intensely want to know how company directors and senior politicians handle the ups and downs of running businesses, states and countries over an extended period. And indeed, your colleagues, from your boss and your boss's boss to your peers, may want to know how you will achieve what you have set out to achieve. Delivery of the complex by making the complex simple, delivery of the simple by making it innovative, delivery of the exciting by creating fervor—all are part of your great speech (and leadership) task.

You don't have to be a five-star general, president of the United States, or a Nobel laureate to speak like a leader. But you do have to be the best you can be. And you have to let yourself shine through in what you say, in whatever circumstances. Let your experience, values, character, vision, even your sense of humor, permeate every word you say and how you say it. When you've said what you have to say as best you can, stop talking and sit down. And this above all else: care very much indeed about your audience. If you don't care about those who are looking at and listening to you—if you don't want what you think is good for them—why are you talking to them in the first place? Think like a leader. Then speak like one.

POINTS TO REMEMBER

- There are a wide variety of quotes and comments on leadership and the responsibility of leadership. Google the word and you'll find a huge source of supply, but choose with care. Only use quotations that you understand and that you unequivocally know that your audiences will understand:
  - "Leadership: the art of getting someone else to do something you want done because he wants to do it." Dwight D. Eisenhower
  - "In times of change, learners inherit the Earth, while the learned find themselves beautifully equipped to deal with a world that no longer exists." Eric Hoffer
  - "I must follow the people. Am I not their leader?" Benjamin Disraeli
  - "Leadership and learning are indispensable to each other." John F. Kennedy
  - "If your actions inspire others to dream more, learn more, do more and become more, you are a leader." John Quincy Adams
  - "I cannot give you the formula for success, but I can give you the formula for failure, which is: try to please everybody." Herbert B. Swope
  - "High sentiments always win in the end. The leaders who offer blood, toil, tears and sweat always get more out of their followers than those who offer safety and a good time. When it comes to the pinch, human beings are heroic." George Orwell
  - "Our chief want is someone who will inspire us to be what we know we could be." Ralph Waldo Emerson
  - "The very essence of leadership is that you have to have vision. You can't blow an uncertain trumpet." Theodore M. Hesburgh

- ○ "Innovation distinguishes between a leader and a follower." Steve Jobs
- Leadership requires oratory whatever the situation or occasion.
- Don't be afraid of leadership or public speaking. Preparation is one of the keys to oratorical success.
- Develop a relationship with your audience—obvious perhaps, but many speakers don't.
- The structure of your speech will add value to your appearance as a leader.
- You don't have to be a president to be a leader. A leader helps others to solve a problem, shows how a problem will be solved and what the world will look like when the problem is solved.

Chapter Six
Sometimes It All
Goes Wrong

"Mistakes are the portals of discovery."
James Joyce (1882–1941)

Mistakes happen. Look at the launch of the Dodge Swinger and the AMC Gremlin, neither of which exactly revved up the automotive world. Look at the launch of New Coke in 1985 which didn't charm the soft drinks market. Similarly, not all presidential speeches are great, so you must choose your models and examples with care. There are bad presidential speeches. For example, Jimmy Carter's "malaise" speech of July 15, 1979, which still elicits disdainful and shocked adjectives among observers and politicians after more than thirty years. There are many who, like Kathleen Hall Jamieson, Professor of Communications at the University of Pennsylvania, thought this speech one of the worst in the presidency's history.

What happened here? Ostensibly about the American energy crisis, Carter's speech did not actually address the crisis until after its 2,000th word. It was a speech that sounded like a dirge, delivered by a president already widely mocked for his low-key and, by and large, dull sermons. It eloquently illuminated complicated problems but offered no real solutions. It directly criticized working people but only indirectly criticized their president, who was after all responsible for coming up with solutions to the energy problem. As it happens, the Carter speech was the end result of a bad-tempered internal debate. Carter was originally meant to give a nationally televised speech on the energy crisis. His advisers argued, and eventually Carter decided to speak instead about the country's moral turpitude. Carter, a devout Southern Baptist, could rarely resist offering a lecture about morals, and so that's what he did; he gave one. He wanted to deliver a speech explaining, as he put it, "what's wrong with America." Unfortunately, that's really all that the speech did. The speech found fault with America and Americans much as a minister would scold his parishioners on a Sunday morning. But this wasn't a Sunday morning sermon to a few hundred people. Carter was addressing a country. He talked of things that would "destroy the social and the political fabric of America." He talked of a "crisis of the American spirit" and he talked of a "growing disrespect for government and for churches and for schools." He talked of a "paralysis and stagnation and drift."

But, actually, that wasn't the main problem at all. The major problem with the speech was not the indictment of average people. Americans, by and large, were indeed unhappy, and one must suppose that Carter had accurately described the nation then. However, after painting a thoroughly depressing picture of the nation's failings and indicating that this would be the status quo for years ahead, Carter offered but one short paragraph's worth of solutions that weren't really solutions at all. "We must face the truth," hectored Carter with pomposity, "and then we can change our course. We simply must have faith in each other, faith in our ability to govern ourselves and faith in the future of this nation." That probably isn't the best way to guide six people listening to a speech or six hundred, let alone six thousand, six million, or even sixty million. Shortly after this speech, given the media's criticism and the public's less than favorable response, Carter asked for the resignation of his entire cabinet. It seemed that he was blaming everyone but himself.

In the 1980 election, Ronald Reagan ran against Carter as a sparkling figure speaking of a dazzling future. Optimism around Reagan was infectious and it was what the public wanted. This was by design of course. In a speech the night before the election, Reagan said, "I find no national malaise. I find nothing wrong with the American people." On January 20, 1981, he was president. Well, apart from the thrills of the political events back then, what can we learn from this? What you must do is make a speech that sets out your content, your aim, and, most important, your plan for how to make your aim come true. Even if you don't know all the answers, say so, but also say what answers you do know. More than that, if you're going to be critical of your audience and its behavior, you'd better know that you're correct and that the examples you have are accurate, but you'd also better know what you're going to suggest is a good corrective path and one into which that audience can buy.

Keep Speeches Short

In 1921, Warren Harding became president of the United States. You may know little about Harding. He's not the best-known president certainly, but his legacy in the speech department is interesting. His maligned inaugural address was a sign of things to come. Harding was surrounded by cabinet scandals; he became famous for odd speech patterns, and finally died of a heart attack while still in office in 1923. More boring than brilliant, his 1921 address went on at yawning length about his philosophy: "I speak for administrative efficiency, for lightened tax burdens, for sound commercial practices, for adequate credit facilities, for sympathetic concern for all agricultural problems, for the omission of unnecessary interference of Government with business, for an end to Government's experiment in business, and for more efficient business in Government administration." The key for any presentation, no matter how many people are in the audience, is to keep it short and always to the point. That means not so short that you can't get the main message across, and not so long that the messages are long lost and those in the audience are not only looking at their watches, but also shaking them, gazing at the second hand on the auditorium clock, and imagining all the things that could be done at home with a paintbrush. There is no rule that says that an executive's speech at a conference or a meeting absolutely must be one and a half hours long, despite what many executives and event managers believe.

The fact of the matter is that presidents don't always speak well, even if the expectation is that they should. The title for this book came from a discussion with the chief executive of a Mumbai-based IT company. The CEO, who had started off at the very bottom rung of the company, had an important speech to make to his shareholders at the company's Annual General Meeting. The company's chairman was not remotely interested in rehearsing or even in involving himself much in the process. The CEO was troubled. "I need to ensure that they (the shareholders) really understand our expansion plans," he said. "If we miss the boat now, then others will replace us as the number one player in this market. I need to come over with leadership, conviction, grace and intelligence. I need to speak like a president." And, safe to say, with help, he did. What he meant, of course, was not that he wanted to speak like an American president necessarily, but like someone who commands respect and who is a senior figure in commerce or politics. But it's also the person who simply wants to speak well and with greatness in front of any audience. So, speaking like a president is all about speaking with confidence, leadership, and belief—as someone whose words will be heard and, most importantly, remembered.

After a brilliant first inaugural address in 1801, Thomas Jefferson was elected once more and offered a strange, dry inaugural speech that was not worthy of the title. He was irritated at the media's attacks over the four years of his previous administration. It's highly likely that he wrote the speech himself and didn't rely on advisers for content or shape. The president was on the defensive and not at his inspirational best: "During this course of administration, and in order to disturb it, the artillery of the press has been leveled against us, charged with whatsoever its licentiousness could devise or dare.

These abuses of an institution so important to freedom and science are deeply to be regretted, inasmuch as they tend to lessen its usefulness, and to sap its safety; they might, indeed, have been corrected by the wholesome punishments reserved and provided by the laws of the several States against falsehood and defamation." Again, and even allowing for the change in language between then and now, the point is clear. You must try hard to leave personal grudges aside. That is difficult, nobody would deny—particularly if the issue you're addressing is burning. But people don't much want to hear about your pet hates particularly if they can't understand where the emotion is from or why you are expressing them. Unless, of course, you're lampooning yourself in a light or an amusing way to make a point, then fine. But avoiding the airing of grudges can be difficult, because if you have the stage it's very easy to feel that the floor is yours to say whatever you like. To a degree, of course, it is. But the deep and warming pleasure of doing that is momentary. Always keep your speech or presentation to the point. When you have finished making your point—stop. Not dead, but come to a conclusion and finish. The best speeches, the greatest speeches, set out their argument, position the counterargument, argue against the counterargument, give their rationale, and conclude. They all relate stories to make a point, and they amuse when amusement is appropriate. More than anything, they take into account the audience—not necessarily what the audience wants to hear, but what the audience is.

Know Your Audiences

In 1869, Ulysses S. Grant perhaps didn't take into account what his audiences were when he made his own inaugural address. He had a tough act to follow, making his presidential inaugural just four years after the famous equivalent given by Abraham Lincoln, but Grant still threw his opportunity far away. This was a time when the United States should have been at peace. However, this war hero chose a hectoring business tone, considering the nation's debts, laws, and flaws, ensuring that any listener would know that he, Grant, didn't like what he found: "To protect the national honor, every dollar of Government indebtedness should be paid in gold, unless otherwise expressly stipulated in the contract. Let it be understood that no repudiator of one farthing of our public debt will be trusted in public place, and it will go far toward strengthening a credit which ought to be the best in the world, and will ultimately enable us to replace the debt with bonds bearing less interest than we now pay." The speech was mostly about problems in commerce, industry, and business. It wasn't at all about how peace might be cherished and enjoyed, how the skies were blue again, and how the future was a chance to rebuild and build. That's what America wanted to hear and learn about.

In the Time Allocated to You, Tell People Some Good Things

There are leaders now around the world—in all walks of commercial or political life—who rarely express pleasure in the fact that something has been or is successful. Strange, but true. People want to hear more than anything else that something is good, that success, no matter how small, has been achieved. That doesn't mean that bad news or difficult information shouldn't be communicated. It does mean that creating a feel good environment, even in times of great hardship, is something that any audience needs. Of course, the weight can tip the balance the other way. What many speakers do is overkill; they express stretched views about how good things are and assume that audiences will believe it even if it's blatantly untrue or not as pervasive as is presented. As a rule, though, audiences can tell the difference between substance and cant.

According to some historians, one of the worst presidential speeches of all time was given by one of the supposedly worst presidents. With the United States already on the road to what would become a harsh civil war, a seemingly strange James

Buchanan, in the delivery of his 1857 inaugural address, essentially ignored the impending conflict, downplayed the growing schism between North and South over slavery, and urged Americans to focus on what he felt were considerably far more important matters: "May we not, then, hope that the long agitation on this subject is approaching its end...Most happy will it be for the country when the public mind shall be diverted from this question to others of more pressing and practical importance." So keep in mind that most audiences have an expectation of what they're about to receive—in a reasonably short space of time. If you give them alternative fare and alternative lengths of time, you need to have an extremely good reason.

At more than 8,000 words, the 1841 inaugural address of distinguished military veteran William Henry Harrison was and still is the longest in inaugural history by a vast margin. It took two hours to deliver in a snowstorm, boring the crowd (such as it remained) and possibly even indirectly killing Harrison, who apparently wore no coat, contracted pneumonia shortly afterward, and died a month into office. He ended his address with this: "Fellow-citizens, being fully invested with that high office to which the partiality of my countrymen has called me, I now take an affectionate leave of you. You will bear with you to your homes the remembrance of the pledge I have this day given to discharge all the high duties of my exalted station according to the best of my ability and I shall enter upon their performance with entire confidence in the support of a just and generous people." He meant well, one must suppose. No matter who you are, keep to the time allocated to you—or less. Many are the occasions when business executives (seriously) overrun during the annual management conference in Dubai or wherever. Running over makes your audience not just bored but angry because you're probably wasting their time and appeasing your own ego. It also shows that you're really not well prepared.

Don't Copy the Bad Behavior of Some Speakers

Some people may think that it's smart to behave strangely onstage and certainly there are some keynote speakers who do behave oddly in the name of being different. Some of these are welcomed because they are allegedly interesting and others are avoided. However, any form of bad behavior or discourtesy can have a detrimental effect. Not that long ago, in September 2009, Libya's Colonel Muammar Abu Minyar al-Gadaffi berated the West for an hour and a half at the United Nations, where he was meant to have spoken for only fifteen minutes. He demanded reform of the UN, which he described as a terrorist organization. He accused the Security Council of being a terrorist body, called for George Bush and Tony Blair to be put on trial for the Iraq war, demanded $7.7 trillion in compensation for the ravages of colonialism in Africa, and pondered whether swine flu was a biological weapon created in a military laboratory. At one point, he even insisted on knowing who was behind the killing of JFK. Paying his first-ever visit to the annual UN General Assembly, the Libyan leader was introduced to the audience of world leaders by the title King of Kings as he took the floor after President Barack Obama. As a finale, Libya's leader tore up a copy of the UN charter in front of the somewhat surprised delegates.

To repeat an important point, keep to the time allocated to you—or less. It's an arrogant stance to ignore time and it smacks of ill-preparation. So if it's you who's doing this, please stop.

Other speeches of note by those who should have delivered better must include the one made by Venezuelan president Hugo Chavez when he addressed the United Nations General Assembly in 2006. Chavez called George W. Bush a "devil" which in itself and in many other places in the world would possibly have been acceptable, but not in the chambers of the General Assembly. Chavez's breach of decorum probably cost Venezuela a position on the Security Council. Similarly and famously, on October 12, 1960, Nikita Khrushchev banged his shoe on the Russian delegate's desk in the

UN to make his point against "American imperialism." Pope Benedict XVI gave a lecture before the University of Regensburg in Germany. His ill-advised and very strange reference to a fourteenth-century Byzantine emperor's remarks on the "evil and inhuman" nature of Islam caused a huge furor and, unsurprisingly, created even more tension between Islam and Christianity.

What Do You Do When Things Go Wrong?

What do you do when a speech goes wrong? First things first—it happens to everyone. Everyone. We all, they all, you all make at least one speech (probably many more) where the thing just does not work. The preparation is inadequate or the tempo is wrong or the audience isn't in the mood. Or the room's too cold or too hot, or the ambiance just isn't right. Or you're talking about the wrong thing. Don't worry about it. Well, yes worry about it, but then fix it. You, just like the presidents of the world, are likely to be embarrassed, humiliated, angry at yourself, angry at the audience, the organizers, the weather, your lunch, the mortgage. You have a few decisions to make. But before you do, it's important to take some deep breaths and perhaps allow yourself to gnash your teeth, but for no more than twenty-four hours. Let's face it—speechmakers (even great ones) can't and won't be in good form all of the time. Even the most prolific and most wonderful speakers occasionally make questionable or just weak or befuddled speeches.

A poor speech is inevitable, especially if you give plenty of them, as is the case with presidents and also teachers, politicians, business executives, and chief executive officers. When the time comes, you'll need to step back from your emotions and begin to ask yourself some questions: What was it exactly that made the speech ineffective or less than great? (Don't use the word "bad"—it's subjective). It's healthy to consider in the harsh light of day real reasons, *specific* reasons, why the speech didn't work. And, please, it will never be the total fault of someone else or the audience. Look at what you did or didn't do. And look at things that may have been outside your control. Were there actually any things over which you had no control, such as the microphone not working and the backup nonexistent? And should you have checked beforehand a bit more thoroughly than you did? Or perhaps you had no opportunity, so you'll be better aware for next time. Was the room too hot (rarely too cold), or was the lighting too much or too little or in the wrong place? Did your PowerPoint not work properly? Did your speech absolutely rely on the PowerPoint? Was the audience particularly hostile for a reason that had nothing to do with you? How do you know? Look, you can shout and scream at or about the people who didn't fix these things. The key lesson for next time is to ensure that you know about your audience and that there are proper technicians to support your speech along with proper backup equipment. When you are famous you'll have people who ensure that these things happen. But even presidents of countries and companies have weird speech days. And presidents and prime ministers have been known to walk into broom cupboards instead of the entrance to the meeting room or stage. Best to know that everything is in hand and the best way to know is to check it all yourself.

There was once a very good senior executive who worked for a retail business based in the United States and Shanghai. He made around four speeches a week to a variety of levels of senior colleagues who hailed from far and wide. After one occasion when his tie microphone failed to work and he had to shout at 280 people with little success, he vowed to check that everything would be working at any occasion in the future. And so he still does. Whether the speech is to a few people or too many, he arranges his travel and schedule so that he can check the sound, the lighting, the PowerPoint—and meet the people organizing the event. He doesn't need to do that anymore because others do it for him, but he still does it anyway. You don't have to adopt an obsessive mentality, but getting into the habit of being comfortable about external factors is very good.

If things have gone wrong, consider whether you should have changed some part of your speech. Could that have made it better? Be ruthless in this process. Did you miss something that was expected by the audience? Was there a topic that you should have covered in more (or less) detail? You will know in your heart of hearts what worked and what didn't. And if you don't, then others will be able to tell you. Ask someone you trust, who speaks the truth no matter how painful. Reasons for delivering less than great speeches are many. Maybe your otherwise great speech was diminished by the fact that the ending should have had more impact—perhaps because you ran out of time—or maybe you should have included some visual to support the piece, or maybe the question and answer session should have been avoided at all costs. Maybe you weren't prepared for the speech. This should probably be the very first question any speaker who delivers less than brilliantly must ask. Were you prepared, did you really engage with the issues, did you simply rehash an old speech, did you try and wing the subject, was it blatant that you didn't know what you were talking about, was there a lack of research, did you know enough about the audience, did you consider the audience not particularly important? Were you too busy with other things to focus on the real subject? If the answer to any of these questions is "yes," then you have work to do.

One of the most prolific speakers on the professional circuit—a retired senior banker—misjudged a particular audience at a conference of about a thousand middle managers. That happens—far too often. He was given a very tough time because he was ill-prepared for that audience. It was embarrassing to see. Instead of forgetting all about the occasion as "one of those unfortunate things," he undertook (publicly) to visit every manager in groups of a hundred to spend time discussing issues of the day. And he was respected for it.

Most speakers who are able to be great speakers know when a presentation has gone badly. Some will never acknowledge fault (although others would contend that admission of fault creates a clearer picture). The best will consider each speech from the point of a number of objectives having been satisfied. As you begin to answer these questions yourself, the paucity in the presentation will begin to appear. Write down all your thoughts as you go through this evaluation process—you'll want to use those notes to ensure that the same negative experience does not occur twice. But don't sweat each issue and don't beat yourself up. Once you have considered where it all went wrong, once you have thought the process through, then forget the whole thing for a while. Don't dwell on postmortems. Take a mental break and reinvent your self-esteem. Clear your thinking. There are many executives around the world who, after delivering a speech that clearly doesn't work, analyze the thing for weeks. This nonsense annoys both colleagues and partners. Having said that, there are many who assume that all their deliveries are superb. Unfortunately, their colleagues and partners tell them the same.

Not All Great Speakers Started Well

Remember, and this is important, many well-known speakers started off their "stage" careers poorly. Mahatma Gandhi, Winston Churchill, Benjamin Disraeli, Benazir Bhutto, Abraham Lincoln, Yitzhak Rabin, Socrates, Jack Welch—all began their public speaking duties with less than powerful speeches. Another thing to remember is that you cannot rewrite your history. If you've made a weak speech for whatever reason, then it's done. Look forward. Every speaker has a rough day. You're not alone. But the best ones press on and learn from their errors. And you can use the poor offering as material for a future speech. Talk about a bad speech during a good one and you'll elicit laughter from your audience. Every person in it will smile, will understand, and will be on your side.

Be Careful What You Say and Do Away From the Stage

Sometimes reputations are lost by what people say away from the cameras or away from a stage. Sometimes politicians and business folk blow their reputations by making comments to colleagues when they think nobody else is listening. There have been dozens of occasions when tie microphones haven't been taken (or switched) off and embarrassing conversations ensue in washrooms, corridors or cars. In the UK 2010 general election, prime minister Gordon Brown still had a live microphone attached after he'd got into his car following a lengthy conversation with a 65-year-old woman who'd asked him a few fairly gentle questions about policies including those relating to immigration. In the car and for all the nation to hear later, he described the pensioner as a "bigoted woman." In August 2006, George Allen was trying to win a convincing reelection as Virginia senator. However, he was caught on video referring to a young Indian-American aide for Democrat Jim Webb as "macaca." "Macaque" is a type of monkey in French and a derogatory word used by former French colonists for the darker skinned natives in the places they conquered. George Allen's mother was French Tunisian and would have known this and likely passed that on to George. The ensuing uproar showed how quickly careers can blow up through thirty embarrassing seconds on YouTube. Another example was when, in September 1988, Michael Dukakis, the Democratic presidential nominee, paid a visit to a General Dynamics plant in Michigan for a photograph opportunity of him atop a tank. This bit of media coverage was meant to promote national security credentials and credibility. Instead, the footage was used in a George H.W. Bush advertisement and made Dukakis look silly. However, the most famous gaffe-prone politician on or off camera, was probably Dan Quayle, the former US vice-President. He was once accused of saying: "I have no problem communicating with Latin American heads of state—though now I do wish I had paid more attention to

Latin when I was at school." This was the Quayle, who once famously spelt "potato" "potatoe," and on another occasion told passing mourners at a funeral to "have a nice day." So, the inference is clear. Yes, we all make mistakes and occasionally say things that we wish we hadn't. Be careful how you behave and what you say onstage and off. It's not just famous people who can end up in trouble. Any great speaker can.

Mind Your Language

Language misinterpretation can be a stumbling block too. Sometimes, it really is hard to know what the customs of a culture or language are, but it is your job to be as accurate and sensitive as possible. Swearing and profanities are never justified and any offensive remarks about any group, strata of society or person are really off limits. Please don't follow the route of TV game show or late night program hosts and assume that anyone or everything is fair game. It's reasonably safe to say that you can be critical of a football team or even a political stance, but just be careful. If in doubt, check or change what you were going to say. President George W. Bush mispronounced the name of the Spanish prime minister, José Maria Aznar, calling him "Ansar" which is Spanish for "goose." On another occasion he went one better than calling Greeks "Grecians" by calling Pakistanis, "Pakis" in front of Pakistan's President Musharraf and that's highly insulting to many Pakistanis. So, the rule of thumb is to check first before you say something you might regret. With difficult names or words, learn how to say them and perhaps write them down phonetically. With the meaning of foreign words, check that the word is correct for your context.

POINTS TO REMEMBER

- Keep any presentation or speech reasonably short and always to the point. Don't fill time.
- Even presidents sometimes make bad speeches. So will you—at least once. Learn from where you went wrong and remember, it's not the end of the world.
- Leave personal grudges and pet hates at home unless they're absolutely relevant to your proposition.
- The best speeches set out their argument, position their counterargument, argue against the counterargument, give their rationale and conclude. They also all take into account what the audience wants or needs.
- People want to hear about good things even when times are tough. In every dark there is some small light. People want to hear of some success even when all around there is failure.
- Some speakers have strange stage habits or create an "act." Others are badly behaved. Always behave well and with great courtesy to everyone.
- Some famous men and women, known for their public speaking, started as weak speakers. Even if you think you're a poor speaker, work at it hard and you will get better.
- Be careful what you say away from the public arena. Your words may come back to haunt you.

Chapter Seven
Time for a Workout: An Oratorical Six-Pack

"A bear, however hard he tries, grows tubby without exercise."
A. A. Milne (1882–1956)

Being a great orator takes work. While there are those who believe that it doesn't and others who have a natural, average talent at telling jokes or making an impromptu speech, real and lasting oratory does take preparation, rehearsal, and practice. In his book, *History of Oratory and Orators: A Study of the Influence of Oratory upon Politics and Literature* (1896), the wonderfully erudite Henry Hardwicke wrote: "The history of the world is full of testimony to prove how much depends upon industry. Not an eminent orator has lived but is an example of it. Yet, in contradiction to all this, the almost universal feeling appears to be, that industry can affect nothing, that eminence is the result of accident, and that everyone must be content to remain just what he may happen to be...For any other art they would have served an apprenticeship and would be ashamed to practice it in public before they had learned it...But the extempore speaker, who is to invent as well as to utter, to carry on an operation of the mind, as well as to produce sound enters upon the work without preparatory discipline, and then wonders why he fails!"

The great myth perpetuated about public speaking is that talent in this area is inherent and inborn and cannot be learned. But our forebears knew better. The great orators of the world from Cicero to Knute Rockne practiced the art of oratory with resolute single-mindedness. They wanted to learn the skill, the craft—and they spent weeks, months, and years honing that skill. We don't have that kind of time any more. Demosthenes is alleged to exemplify the drive for perfection particularly well. He would, it is said, go to the sea and recite orations louder than the waves. He is also said to have then isolated himself in a cave for weeks on end to rehearse and practice oratory. In order to avoid being tempted to leave the cave before he was ready, he shaved off half the hair on his head, knowing he would be subjected to giggling abuse were he to show his face in that state. In an attempt to improve his pronunciation, he recited speeches while his mouth was filled with pebbles—probably not a practice one would want to emulate now. It is said that Demosthenes practiced his speaking in front of a mirror on a daily basis, improving any defect in his delivery or body language. He had a nervous tic of raising one shoulder while he spoke. So to correct this, he hung a sword above that shoulder that would cut him if he raised it. But, of course, no one is suggesting that you do this (and it's by no means certain that Demosthenes did), but to be a great speaker, you have to *want* to be a great speaker and that does mean practice.

Take Note of Great Orators

Caring about speech, words, and expressing ideas is fascinating and essential to anyone who wants to speak with greatness. "There is no true orator who is not a hero," said Ralph Waldo Emerson in his chapter 'Eloquence' in *Letters and Social Aims* (1875). William Jennings Bryan, Democratic Party presidential nominee in 1896, 1900, and 1908, was a brilliant orator and also a successful lawyer and secretary of state in President Woodrow Wilson's administration. One of the most popular and successful orators in American history, Bryan was noted for a rich, deep, powerful voice and a speech delivery of eloquence and style that demanded attention. That didn't happen overnight either. Because he fought for (and had faith in) basic, good values, Bryan was often called by the press "The Great Commoner." He certainly defended the modest trader and those whose voices were otherwise unheard. For everyone who makes a good or great speech or presentation, there is a moment when the speech counts, when its point is so valid and clear and when you know, just know, that the message has hit home. Some people call Bryan's *Address to the Chicago Democratic National Convention*, given on July 8, 1896, one such. Many regard it as the most famous ever in American political history. In closing the debate on the party platform, Bryan's strong words hit the mark with the crowd. Bryan criticized the gold standard and advocated inflating the currency by the free coinage of silver, a measure popular among the debt-ridden farmers championed by Bryan. The carefully prepared and brilliantly delivered speech is a cornerstone of economic populism. He said: "The individual is but an atom; he is born, he acts, he dies; but principles are eternal, and this has been a contest over a principle." He also said, "You shall not press down upon the brow of labor this crown of thorns, you shall not crucify mankind upon a cross of gold."

Bryan's speech model was to build a case. It's a good policy. Build your case, attack what needs attacking, but always have solutions. Attacking with no substantial case may make you feel good, but eventually achieves little. Remember what happened to Jimmy Carter. Too many reasonable speeches fall flat because they offer no new thinking, no solutions. They only criticize, attack, and offer nothing. Bryan attacked the widely held view that gold was the only reliable currency. He admitted openly to speaking out for small businesses and farmers. His speech extolled their virtues. He railed against a government that, he claimed, ignored the smallholder and favored large corporations in a way that was ruining the country and destroying the hopes and aspirations of the average working man and woman. But he didn't just complain; he had suggestions, and he put them forward forcibly and logically. The result of the speech was extraordinary. Bryan was nominated by the delegates as their candidate for president. And he was only thirty-six.

Be generous. In his speech, Bryan removed personality from the contest. This was and is a healthy technique. If a speech becomes personal, the danger is that audiences won't warm to it. They might, depending on their view of the individual or individuals, but too much spite or invective can cause a discomfort reflecting poorly on you, the speaker. Politicians make this mistake too often and at their peril. Bryan said, "I would be presumptuous, indeed, to present myself against the distinguished gentlemen to whom you have listened if this were mere measuring of abilities; but this is not a contest between persons. The humblest citizen in all the land, when clad in the armor of a righteous cause, is stronger than all the hosts of error. I come to speak to you in defense of a cause as holy as the cause of liberty—the cause of humanity." Bryan was thought to be a celebrity, who might be better known for his vibrant and vivid personality and oratorical skill considerably more so than his political outlook, beliefs, and action. He is given credit for making the Democratic Party strong in opposition and powerful in government. It was his oratorical prowess that set a speaking style from which politicians thereafter have learned and benefited. Those who want to discover excellent speech structure, great language, and wonderful resonance that truly leaps from the page have but to read Bryan's speeches.

Good Character Sounds Wimpy, But is Important

No grammatical parsley or oratorical flourish can add as much garnish to a speech as good character. The very hint of hypocrisy will doom even the most eloquent speech. You see that every day from politicians of every hue around the world, apart from rare occurrences such as Bill Clinton's close call. When you are honest, direct, consistent, and committed to your argument, then sincerity shines through. This may sound overly idealistic, but it's true. Audiences want entertainment, yes, but they primarily want words to which they can adhere. People in audiences are not stupid. They will feel the depth of your commitment and will listen far more intently than they would if they knew what you are saying was claptrap. Cicero put it well in his *De Oratore* (written, don't forget, in 55 B.C.): "In an orator, the acuteness of the logicians, the wisdom of the philosophers, the language almost of poetry, the memory of lawyers, the voice of tragedians, the gesture almost of the best actors, is required. Nothing therefore is more rarely found among mankind than a consummate orator." That broad umbrella under which the orator sits must necessitate learning. Not the kind advanced in academia necessarily, but in order to appeal to your audiences, your speeches must be filled with allusions to the characters, events, and artistic expressions of history and of your time and culture. You must keep abreast of and, where appropriate, refer to current events, music (not just what you like either), theater (ditto), movies (ditto once more), well-known personalities, stories of the day, what happened in well-known soaps last night, religion, human nature, science, literature, and poetry. Read newspapers. Listen to the radio. Watch great films. Read at least a paragraph of great literature each day. Do not simply frequent blogs and Web sites that flatter your current views. A great orator must be aware of the counterarguments your critics will raise and deftly address and defuse them before anyone else can. Always think of counterarguments to what you are going to say. This is critical for any question and answer sessions which may be planned or unplanned. It's also critical because if you posit views against counterarguments, then you will smartly remove the carpet from under the feet of any (quiet or loud) dissenters in the audience.

Keep learning. Take as your coaches and mentors all the great orators of the past. Read their speeches. Study the way in which they constructed their sentences, how the placement and arrangement of words build rhythm, how the choice of words and stories creates vivid imagery. Examine how each line flows into the next, how the lines are distinct and yet together compose a cohesive, unified whole. They won't all press your buttons, and there's no reason why they all should. But persevere. Also listen to great speeches. Listen to where the orators pause for effect, where a voice rises and falls. Ponder what makes certain sections electrifying and others captivating. And ponder why some parts might be perceived as downright boring or dull to today's audiences.

Prepare and Rehearse

If you're nervous about speaking in public (and many people are), continued rehearsal will give you confidence and make the experience a great deal less traumatic. If you're a confident public speaker, don't be tempted to skimp on the preparation. It can be easy to think that because speaking is something we do all the time, we don't need to practice it. Somehow it seems obvious that we'd need to rehearse before performing in public in any other way—singing, dancing, playing an instrument, acting, doing a magic trick—even telling a joke, particularly telling a joke maybe. And yet when we're faced with making a speech, we can fall into the trap of thinking we can improvise. Even if you prepare minimally, still prepare. Once you've written your speech or presentation in your head, make a bullet-point summary of it. If you leave it as a full script, it will be almost impossible for you, when the time comes, not to read it. This is not necessarily to say that a speech should never be read, but if it is, you have to be very good at presenting, so that the process looks and sounds as if you're not reading your speech. Bullet points remind you what you want to say, but force you to say it rather than read it. Then when you deliver your speech out loud, use your bullet points as prompts. If you find you're not saying it as well as you prepared it, read through your full script a few more times to help you memorize it. What you're aiming at is a delicate balance between reciting and improvising that requires all your acting skills. You should sound as if you're making the speech for the first time, and here lies a problem for many speakers who "do the circuit." The ennui begins to show after a while. Think of a stage actor who must perform the same role night after night. It is part of the actor's job to make each performance new, or the audience would get up, walk out, and demand their money back.

Don't Be Boring

Never bore your audience. You may not know if you are being boring, but if you are aware of your audience, then there is less likelihood that you will bore anyone. Some speakers simply don't care if they bore their audiences or not. Here's an essential technique to improve your speech and avoid the boredom trap. It's the compare and contrast technique. This is one of those old oratory devices that has been used since the times of Cicero. A contrast (or juxtaposition) is where two viewpoints are placed close to each other for effect. Instead of giving out a list of facts, you compare them from different angles. Here is a memorable example. John F. Kennedy wanted to encourage American citizens to become more active in helping the country. He could have said, "We all need your help," and it would have been forgotten two days later. Instead he used a contrast and said, "Ask not what your country can do for you, ask what you can do for your country." Shakespeare supplies another example. In *Hamlet*, the great playwright could have written, "I think that I might kill myself." Instead he wrote, "To be or not to be, that is the question." He then goes on to compare "Whether 'tis nobler in the mind to suffer / The slings and arrows of outrageous fortune, / Or to take arms against a sea of troubles, / And by opposing end them?" There are many other examples of contrasts in literature. One of the most famous is the brilliant start of *A Tale of Two Cities* by Charles Dickens: "It was the best of times, it was the worst of times, it was the age of wisdom, it was the age of foolishness, it was the epoch of belief, it was the epoch of incredulity, it was the season of Light, it was the season of Darkness, it was the spring of hope, it was the winter of despair, we had everything before us, we had nothing before us, we were all going direct to Heaven, we were all going direct the other way." The contrasts are obvious and present an extraordinary, powerful, and utterly memorable beginning to the book.

To begin using the device in your speeches, you simply need to bring some comparisons and contrasts to bear. For example, "On one hand we have the...and on the other hand we are..." or perhaps something like, "The situation puts us between a rock and a hard place. Let's take a look at both." Be careful of such smart phrases, however. Use them sparingly, otherwise your audience will think you are too pleased with yourself.

To structure a speech, you can use the compare and contrast structure to great effect. So if your speech is on China, you could say, "China has a population of 1.347 billion. A stronger statement would be "China has a population of 1.347 billion, which is over four times as much as that of the 300 million or so in the United States." Said Benjamin Franklin, "Content makes poor men rich; discontent makes rich men poor." FDR declared, "There is nothing to fear but fear itself." You'll quickly think of your own, but again, be sparing and be deft.

Great speeches are often sparing and deft. On the night he was made the new president of the United States, Barack Obama delivered a speech that might have seemed like it came off the cuff. Of course, this was as well planned and well rehearsed as any and might end up being classed as one of the greatest speeches. The power of three is a technique that has been used often in oratory. It is used because it flows nicely, because it is enough for the listener to absorb without feeling overloaded, and because it feels complete. It sounds good. Obama uses the power-of-three technique several times in this speech: "It's been a long time coming, but tonight, *because of what we did on this day, in this election, at this defining moment*, change has come to America." And the crowd roared, for here was poetry. Obama not only used the power of three, but he also involved his audience with the use of the phrase "what *we* did." This makes the celebration shared—not his, but "theirs" and "ours." More than that, it deliberately involves and engages his television audience. They feel successful too, and included. Using the word "we" gives the feeling that Obama (and those who voted for him) are united, that they have succeeded in a venture. Take a look at this second example from the same speech: "If there is anyone out there who still doubts that America is a place *where all things are possible*; *who still wonders if the dream of our founders is alive in our time*; *who still questions the power of our democracy*, tonight is your answer." Not only does it use the power of three again, but it also has repetition, another useful tool for getting the point across and emphasizing an important part of what you have to say, without being dull. On the subject of useful tools, and the involvement of the people, look at this part of the Obama speech: "It's the answer spoken by young and old, rich and poor, Democrat and Republican, black, white, Hispanic, Asian, Native American, gay, straight, disabled and not disabled—Americans who sent a message to the world that we have never been just a collection of individuals or a collection of Red States and Blue States: we are, and always will be, the United States of America." This works on two levels. Firstly, we are made to believe that he's speaking to us all—he has recognized who you are and who I am; the address is therefore personal. Secondly, by grouping everyone together, he has once again created a feeling of kinship and teamwork working.

Further into his speech, Obama gives reference to events that have happened in the past—the abolition of black slavery, Pearl Harbor, times before women had rights—each one of these references will have touched one kind of nerve or another with the people of America and will have given a connection between those people and their new president. So, to be a great speaker you have to be able to do three things: connect with your audience, make listeners feel as if you are addressing them as individuals, and make them believe in something.

But what makes one person's speech stand out and become remembered as great—so great that people study it long after it is delivered, even after the cause has been forgotten? Or, to put it differently, what makes another person's speech last only as long as the time it takes to deliver it, forgotten as soon as the audience leaves the room, and of zero importance once audience members are on the aircraft home? Is there a single aspect of speechmaking that really is absolutely essential to its success? Is it belief? Well, almost anyone can stand in front of a crowd of people and talk about their chosen topic, but not everyone can make it believable. Belief is so very important. You've seen the bored, lukewarm executive run through appalling PowerPoint graphs and graphics in a monotone, dry, disconnected voice. Why? Because it's accepted or acceptable? Because his or her boss knows no better? Because, it's seen as "all right"? We have such great opportunities to tell our stories, whether they are about sales figures, one's daughter, a lost friend, a found friend, a new piece of business, an election promise, or Sally Shoesmith, but we squander golden, bright opportunities. This is not always our fault. Circumstances fight against us, but actually that's not an excuse. If you want to make a great speech or presentation, you do have to *really* want to make it. There has to be a passion that drives great speeches. Great orators show that whatever they're talking about means more to them than anything else. It's a very good place to begin.

Preparation and Planning

When preparing a presentation, there is clearly (at least in most cases) a reasonable amount of time spent on researching the subject and on planning how to present it, but there are probably four major points to consider when preparing your speech:

- Why are you presenting?
- Why are *you* presenting? (Short straw? Or are you the acknowledged expert?)

- What is the presentation about? (*Really* about? Not sure? Some doubt? Then make sure now.)
- To whom are you presenting? (What are they? What level? What are their expectations? What do they know?)

"Why?' and "What?' are probably the two aspects that come highest on the list when in the writing stage. Think logically. Write down what you absolutely know your audience will want to hear. Start from that point. Do not under any circumstances spend the first thirty minutes in any speech telling people what they already know. They'll hate you for it. By all means summarize that element, but in about two minutes flat. People in audiences can make huge quantum leaps. They "get" stuff. Sometimes speakers explain too much. Basic language is fine. Basic language that shows belief is the order of any speech. Keep to facts. Know your facts. There are many instances when highly respected academics or presenters have been caught out because they're economical with the truth. That's not the same as acknowledging that you think that something is so or that something is approximate.

PowerPoint

PowerPoint is overused and is probably one of the core causes of dry, dull speeches. Many people use it is a crutch and they think that the PowerPoint material is all they need. The view is that it will do. The vast majority of great speakers didn't and don't use PowerPoint. Many people will be tempted—or coerced—into using the program. With care it *can* make your presentation easier to understand and can also help you discipline your thoughts into more logical, bite-sized chunks. But if your presentation is boring, PowerPoint won't make it interesting. It might even make it worse if you use it as a substitute for planning, thought, style, and content. PowerPoint, as its name suggests, is a powerful tool. And as with other powerful tools, things can go horribly wrong if you don't know how to use it.

This has little to do with the basic functions, with which you're presumably familiar, or you have an assistant who is. But the fact is that there are many ways to ruin a presentation and PowerPoint is one of them. A monotone delivery, lack of preparation and boring content are killers, but perhaps the most common way to ring the death knell over your presentation is to have too many intersecting circles, tiny labels, or flying arrows on the screen. This has the effect of scrambling audience members' brains while they try to divide their attention between listening, reading, or deciphering—and doing none of it very well. It's also a pain to sit through for one slide, let alone a whole presentation of confusing slides. Why do people do it? You might think you're actually being helpful by putting stuff on the screen, thinking you're reinforcing the message. The opposite is the case. Another reason could be laziness: this can range from not bothering to make the presentation more interesting, to not picturing the effect on the audience. But whatever the reason, it's not a great idea to have too many words on screen and then to read them aloud. That's just dull.

So what's the solution? One answer is, unsurprisingly, to cut down the number of words. PowerPoint has a whole range of other options, including visuals, diagrams, and even different colors for words. Use them; think about how they could help cut down or eliminate big chunks of text. PowerPoint is not there to give the audience a good read (even if they can properly see the tiny text or decipher an odd font). PowerPoint is only ever there to support what a speaker says. Be brave. With PowerPoint less is most definitely much more. As a possibility, having (very) few words on screen allows you to react to or expand on them and even make the presentation more interactive by asking questions. It's easy to have two or three words up on screen and talk around them without losing the audience. Sometimes, it can be argued (although not very convincingly), that you need to have lots of words on screen, for example, legal phrasing where every word is vital. There is an argument for leaving any detail to be dished out at the end of a presentation in the form of a handout or, conversely, to be given out or put on a Web site prior to the speech. Also, if there simply has to be stuff on screen that the audience must read in order for your argument to work, then stop talking for a minute and let people read it. But there are very few instances where that would be a good move. Did Cicero, Churchill, or Kennedy use PowerPoint? Does Bill Gates? PowerPoint is much like a computer. It's got more devices on it than most of us can ever use or know how to even if we so wanted. You can do lots of different things with it, and there are specialists who use it brilliantly. Get one of those people onside and ensure that this person understands the nature of your speeches. But just because you can do things with the device doesn't mean that you should. In fact, the smart presenters would never consider using certain of its facilities. They tend to be the ones whose presentations are interesting, fun, and absorbing—unlike those who put their audiences to sleep despite the myriad of colors and shapes. Take tables of data, for instance. There's no difficulty putting the most complex matrix up on the screen. But it's almost never a wise move. People won't be able to read the figures from the back of the room; and those who can read them from the front will get lost trying to follow them and wish they were sitting at the back or enjoying a sandwich somewhere. Tables are death to a presentation.

Remember, if people are reading, they're absolutely not listening. If you're standing at the front reading something out while words are on the screen, the audience's attention will be torn two ways and the screen's likely to win (momentarily anyway). It's good to have no words at all on some slides. A (very) simple diagram, picture, or photograph can make a point more powerfully than any number of PowerPoint words. Contrast a presenter saying, "Last year, our sales rose by 43.6 percent, with March and September producing the best months" and another presenting those facts in a graph. The key points are grasped almost instantly via the verbal way—and much more dramatically. Many presenters seem to forget that audiences have more than one sense. It's fine to stimulate those other senses—so long as you remember that vision will always win out. And PowerPoint is great for running short, effective video clips, for example, complete with arresting sound. Short video or graphics clips that reinforce your argument can really give your audiences a buzz. Used correctly, PowerPoint is a great tool. It can enliven presentations and make your points really stand out. Don't rely on it, though. Be selective of its facilities and use them carefully.

Watch Your Time

Nothing kills a presentation more than going on too long. Twenty minutes is a good rule of thumb. Yes, really. Leave people wanting more. Twenty minutes is what people can, by and large, grab in one serving, and unless you're briefing troops for battle, there seems little reason in speaking longer. You shouldn't need to. Imagine what it would be like if there were ten of you speaking at a conference. How would people remember what you said, particularly if you were speaking at slot number nine? That has to be another driver for your content and delivery. People tend to remember only three things— three messages, three arguments, three reasons, three anything. Work out the three messages that you want your audience to take away and structure your presentation around them. And don't forget to rehearse; that will help you keep your speech to a reasonable length. Also, try very hard indeed not to look at your watch. It insults the audience and it gives the impression that either you want to be elsewhere or you know that you haven't finished and your lucky listeners have another forty minutes of you. The best thing is to carry a small travel clock with you and put it on the lectern or table.

Taking the Job of Speaking Seriously

Let's suppose you're a pianist. You're booked to give a concert of a great but challenging piano piece. You show up on time, you're immaculately dressed, and you certainly look the part. You flick a lock of hair back from your forehead. You flex your fingers. You're ready, but you're not. Unfortunately, you have not practiced that piece. You plan to play it straight from the score. It probably doesn't take much imagination to see that this performance is not likely to be a hit. If it's memorable, it will be for all the wrong reasons. You're in a similar situation when you give a presentation. How good you are will depend a lot on your preparation and practice. Great performances truly don't happen by chance. A stand-up comedian doesn't do his or her act because he can recall only a few jokes.

To help you, it's a good idea to video a few of your performances. Nobody will mind. Once you've got your video, what do you do with it? The answer is twofold. First, you review it. The chances are that it will tell you dozens things about you that you never even realized. Does that monotone voice make you cringe? Introduce some variation. Are your arms are fixed stiffly to your sides? Add some gestures for emphasis. (Watch any politician and you'll see how important gestures can be when speaking in public. Having said that, they are not always cognizant of this fact!) How's your posture? If you're slouching, stooping, or standing with sagging shoulders, straighten up and remember to do this when you're on stage, not so that you look as if you have some ironmongery stuffed down your jacket but relaxed and in charge. Are you too serious? Smile, maybe tell a joke or two. And you probably never realized how little eye contact you made. Watching your video will reveal many things that you're doing wrong, but that's excellent—because you can then fix 'em before you give your next presentation. The second thing to do is to get someone else to review your video. An independent viewer is likely to spot things you can't or don't. This may be painful, but remember, it's (or should be) constructive criticism. As long as the weak areas can be improved—and almost all of them can be—you can learn a whole lot from someone else's (honest) comments. If you're planning to make a career of giving presentations and speaking in public, your video can even be used as a sort of CV. Videoing your presentation will definitely improve your performance. It will also make you more confident.

With confidence (not arrogance) comes an ability to use what you have—your voice, your accent, your movements and the way you walk across the stage and make eye contact. Try to keep your presentation easy on the ear and on the eye: add pauses, gestures, intonations, and so on. You may well find that some sections work well presented in a certain way, while others work better another way. Preparation and rehearsal will help you get a natural flow to your presentation. This may not make your presentation perfect or indeed great—but it will improve it, probably by a big margin. After all, would you rather make your mistakes on your own and fix them—or make them in front of your important and critical audience?

Many people dread giving a presentation. The reason is not hard to find; presentations require skill sets that many of us just have not built up in our day-to-day work. So we might be an expert IT person, or know everything there is to know about recruitment or dinosaurs or the politics of Delhi or the machinations of the World Bank. But there's no reason why we should be any good at presentations unless we make them. Unless you're a professional presenter, you might be called upon to do just a handful of these a year—perhaps fewer. To be a great presenter might require you to set aside hundreds of hours for practice. Compare that to what most people actually spend on preparing for a speech and you'll see that there's something of a shortfall.

Memorable Oratory Comes From Preparation

Lincoln spent weeks on his very short Gettysburg address. Churchill spent an hour preparing each minute of set-piece speeches. He never forgot breaking down in the House of Commons, confused and artless, back in 1904, reduced to humiliated silence. So he wrote and prepared and rehearsed. Fix your audience, know who they are, prepare, prepare some more, and deliver.

At his inauguration, Barack Obama used some Churchillian full stops: "The capital was abandoned. The enemy was advancing. The snow was stained with blood." Tony Blair, who, when in office as the UK's prime minister, always left out essential bits of grammar and structure in most speeches, might have said: "Capital abandoned. Enemy advancing. Snow stained with blood." It would have slid down smoothly—but then slipped away from the memory. When Hitler's contemporaries in Britain and the United States saw newsreels of his speeches, they beheld a gesticulating, wild-eyed man in a uniform apparently raging uncontrollably. Today, as then, such film clips create the image of a madman. However, like any brief bite of sound (dangerous things), these snippets give a false impression. Hitler was certainly a megalomaniac, power hungry and obsessed with racial purity. His speeches, far from revealing his insanity, are examples of his careful, clear-sighted planning, and intelligent (if Machiavellian) strategies in communication and audience manipulation. He trained himself to become an orator. His first public utterance, a fiery rebuttal from the back row of a point made in a Worker's Party meeting, so impressed the party leader, Anton Drexler, that Drexler sought Hitler out and recruited him shortly afterward to become propaganda manager. As spokesman for the party, Hitler soon made a bid for the leadership and changed its name to the National Socialist (Nazi) Party. This is not a history lesson. The point is that great orators (no matter what the purpose of their oratory) prepare and rehearse. Hitler did.

POINTS TO REMEMBER

- A contrast (or juxtaposition) is where two viewpoints are placed close to each other for effect. Instead of giving out a list of facts, you compare them from different angles. Here is a memorable example. John F. Kennedy wanted to encourage American citizens to become more active in helping the country. He could have said, "We all need your help," and it would have been forgotten two days later. Instead he used a contrast and said, "Ask not what your country can do for you—ask what you can do for your country."

- Being an orator takes work—preparation and rehearsal, just as you would if you were acting on stage, singing, or playing a piece of music—anywhere in fact where you might perform in front of an audience.

- People are not born with an oratorical skill or a talent for public speaking. All great speakers prepared and rehearsed.

- Consider carefully what goes into your speeches. Explore the ideas of others and listen to and read great speeches.

- Like William Jennings Bryan, for example, build your case, attack what needs attacking but always have solutions to suggest.

- Be generous to others but keep personality conflicts out of your speeches. If your speeches become personal there's a danger that audiences won't like it or you.

- People in audiences like good character—not a creepy goody two shoes—but someone who is decent and clearly honest. Any hint of hypocrisy or the telling of untruths can doom even the best speech.

- Read newspapers, watch great and famous movies, see good theater, find out what's going on in soaps and well-known TV programs, listen to and know about modern music, know what advertising is in and what is out, know about new products, understand the current political situation wherever you are, know the news of the day, understand how to pronounce brands, products and new things that those in the audience will understand how to pronounce.

- The rule of three is a powerful oratorical device. It sounds good and contains just enough information for a listener to absorb. Harnessing the power of the rule of three allows you to express concepts more completely and emphasize any argument. Some good examples abound: "We can not dedicate—we can not consecrate—we can not hallow—this ground." From Abraham Lincoln's Gettysburg Address. From the same speech: "Government of the people, by the people, for the people." The phrase "wine, women, and song" is another good example as is a piece from Steve Jobs's Stanford Commencement Address (2005): "It means to try and tell your kids everything you thought you'd have the next ten years to tell them in just a few months. It means to make sure everything is buttoned up so that it will be as easy as possible for your family. It means to say your goodbyes."
- To be a great speaker you have to do three things: connect with your audience, make listeners feel as if you're addressing them as individuals and make them believe in something.

Chapter Eight
Who Cares About
Audiences Anyway?

**"I went on all over the States, ranting poems to
enthusiastic audiences that, the week before, had
been equally enthusiastic about lectures on
Railway Development or the Modern Turkish Essay."**
Dylan Thomas (1914–1953)

There is no short cut. Preparation. It helps of course if what you have
to say is interesting to your audience. But it's preparation and
rehearsal that will make you good and then great. That and
understanding your audience. People have gathered (maybe Sally
Shoesmith's eleven or maybe Central Park's eleven thousand) to
hear you speak on a specific issue, and they will expect to get
something out of it immediately. Long gone are the days when the
preacher or the politician could develop his theme in a long,
interesting, perhaps convoluted way, reaching the peroration after
some considerable time. We are all short of time and patience these
days, and unless you are a professional entertainer or you own the
company or are indeed a president of something or somewhere,
then the expectation is that what you have to say will need to be
succinct and immediate. And you, the speaker, want to have an
immediate effect on your audience. You want to know that there is
approbation—that you're on the right track. The purpose of your
speech is to get the response you want.

Your Speech Needs to Get a Reaction

Most speeches invite audiences to react in one or all of three ways: feel, think, or act. For example, eulogies encourage an emotional response from the audience, lectures stimulate listeners to think about a topic from a different or new perspective, and senior executives expect certain behavior or actions as a result of what they have to say. As you consider your speaking purpose, ask yourself these questions:

- What do you want the audience to learn or do? Be precise in your thinking about this. Be specific and highly focused.
- Think about your case or argument. Why do you want the audience to agree with you? Again, the more specific the better.
- If you think audience members will already agree with you, or if you know unequivocally that they do, why then are you giving the speech?
- How can your audience benefit from what you have to say? If your purpose is to get a certain response from your audience, you must know what sort of people are in it. You shouldn't imagine that they are what they're not.
- Are you merely repeating a speech that you've made a hundred times before? Why? And are you really sure that this audience is exactly the same as the preceding one hundred?
- Are you planning, as an introduction, to bore people rigid by telling them what they already know? Senior executives in banks, pharmaceutical companies, or high street retail outlets please take note. Politicians, even senior ones, who should know much, better sit up too.
- What do people in the audience have in common? Think about age, interests, background, job, experience, ethnicity, and gender. You may not get to know some of these things

with great precision, but if you always insist on a good brief, then you'll get to know more than you did. If you don't get a proper brief, then you have every right to be concerned.

- Will the people in the audience know as much about your topic as you, or will you be introducing them to new ideas? Will they know *more* than you, in which case are you talking about the right subject? Have you understood the task? Did you listen properly? Did read the briefing notes? Did you realize that the word "you" is missing from the previous question?

- Why are these people listening to you? What are they looking for? What have you got that they want? Are you special?

- What level of detail will be effective for them?

- What tone will be most effective in conveying your message?

- What might offend or alienate the audience?

- What will make people smile or laugh? Do you know which TV program or movies they might like? News sources they might read or to which they will listen? Current affairs stories they may know about? Do they know the people of whom you'll be speaking? There's no point in mentioning anybody unless you put them into a context.

Only Connect

Even though it might be blindingly obvious, it's a good idea to explain to your audience why your topic is important. You could begin by telling people how and why you considered your purpose and how you came to speak to them in the first place, that is, why you are there before them. You'll recall that in *Howards End*, that great novel by E. M. Forster, the preface page has two words which are prophetic within the book's meaning: "Only Connect." The phrase is also apposite when considering the importance of engaging with an audience. And it's your job to do that. So many speakers come off stage and say, "Well, they weren't very interested were they?" Or, "That joke works every time. Don't understand why these guys didn't laugh." Or, "I normally connect right away with people like this." If the people in the audience weren't interested, that's predominantly down to you. Certainly they may be thinking about their next meeting, and certainly they may be considering the best way to get from wherever you are to the airport, certainly they may have their own presentation about which to worry, and certainly they may be wondering about credit card debt or lots of other things, but the commitment to audience engagement is down to you, just as it is with anyone on any stage anywhere.

For the best audience engagement (again no matter whether that audience comprises six or six thousand), it's also important to ensure that you connect your material to related or larger issues, especially those that may be important to your audience and, importantly, to the conference or overall event—if that's applicable. Never forget that unless you are the only presenter or speaker, you are part of a whole. It's your duty to ensure that you know how you fit into that whole. Of course, some conference organizers won't have a clue how you fit into the whole and neither will the conference's architect or company's CEO. Force the issue. You have to know. And once you understand what your audience is about and like, you will be in a better position to know how to prepare your speech and material to support your speech or presentation. Suffice it say, if you don't understand your listeners, then your speech is unlikely to work or be well received. Put yourself in their position. What would press your buttons? What would float your particular boat? What would excite, interest, and focus you if you were listening to you? A successful presenter is more than just a fact dispenser—he or she really knows how to communicate with an audience; she or he must become someone to whom people will listen.

The great speaker in business, just as in the political arena, is the one who can make people hear the facts and believe the message. You know that there are a myriad other aspects besides audience comprehension that come together to make a speech or speaker successful: confidence, phraseology, body language, wit, visual support, stage management, technical provision, organization, and all the other skills that go into the act of public speaking. But understanding what makes an audience tick is up there at the top of the list. Any audience wants to know and to feel that you know what you're talking about. People in audiences also want to feel that you look the part, that you respect them and acknowledge their situation and views. They want to have sufficient information to make a considered judgment about what you say. They want to weigh up your views and either reject them or accept them. They want to be clear about any necessary action. They most definitely do not want to be confused by overly scientific or technical explanations or jargon. They really don't want to be lost in your complicated speech structure (or lack of a clear one). They don't want to be treated to condescension or made to struggle to understand inappropriate language or humor that floats off to the ether or sinks like lead. They do not want to be forced to make enormous leaps to relate what you say to their own circumstances or experience.

Remember, audiences *can* make huge leaps in understanding thereby making it unnecessary for you to spell out every single step. Audiences can connect with what you have to say very fast, provided it's clearly expressed. However, there are situations where some speakers assume that audiences will make cosmic leaps with them, the outcome of which is not actually blindingly clear. If the audience members fall into a dark pit of confusion, and if you've led them there, then each member will care nothing for anything else other than breathing clean air and seeing some familiar architecture in sunlight. And neither does any listener want to listen to someone whose lack of preparation makes it clear they have no respect for the audience. It is very obvious, but very important, to remember that as the presenter or speaker, you are there for your audience members, and you must earn the right by proving your credibility to be standing in front of them. If you accept that it is indeed your audience, you have to ensure that the people in it really *are* your audience and that needs to be foremost in your thinking, planning, and delivery.

Inspire Your Audiences

Your job as a speaker is to inspire the people in an audience and make as many of those people as possible feel totally positive about themselves. Many people listening to the inspirational speech given by you will carry home a feeling of belief. That's true of the Wednesday sales meeting with Sally Shoesmith and colleagues or the national conference with two thousand managers from around the country, who have traveled far and wide to listen to you. Inspiring speeches are just as necessary when times are hard, money is short, opportunities are less, and people are really seeking meaning in each walk of life. Great speakers are good at the art of inspiring people and making them look at life with a newfound belief and enthusiasm. People will look to you to give inspiring speeches to which an attentive audience will relate. You will speak convincingly about whatever subject so that the people listening to you are inspired by what you say. Your speech will not give a lot of boring advice. Your speech will be interesting, innovative, challenging, and exciting, and it will inspire people to think differently or to have their opinions reinforced. All of these things may be present and correct, and still there's an element missing perhaps. If you are having difficulties connecting with your audiences, then it's likely that you're not making the audience the hero of your story. Style is important, the ability to present professionally is important, but if you want people in the audience to be engaged while listening to your presentation, then you need to make them the heroes and heroines. Also, you will never connect with your audience unless your speech has spirit, no matter what its purpose. A spirited speech engages an audience because it makes its members feel that they are enabled to face a new challenge, that they made a correct decision, or it reaffirms the action that has taken them to where they are today.

One problem of course is that many speakers in politics, business, or commerce use the platform to demonstrate how much smarter they are than the audience, how much cooler they are, or how accomplished they are as a speaker. Doing that is wrong, and it will eventually kill your spirit as a speaker. It will also murder any engagement you have with your audiences. Don't be smug and don't be condescending. Neither have a place in public speaking. You're on the platform to affirm or change the beliefs of the audience members or propel them to take action on some point that you are making. You're there to explain, reinforce views, to give hope, to make them feel better about something, to tell them how to do better in something—whatever.

Giving a great speech is about embracing the listeners with your heart, validating them, and making them, not you, the hero. As you write your next speech, ask yourself, is this for me or is this for the audience? If it's for the audience, how can you present in such a way that makes your audience the hero? Show that you care more about the audience than you do yourself. The other factor here is that if you consider your audience more than yourself, then you'll make fewer mistakes. There will be less of the white-knuckled grip of the lectern, the awkward what-to-do-with the hands, or the nervous swinging of the laser pointer that may accidentally blind the front row from time to time. There will be less of the gap fillers such as "um," "ah," "so," and the one word or phrase that will become the bête noire of your speech because you'll repeat it ad nauseam. What is that word? Not a clue because it'll be yours and awful. Some say "some such thing" repeatedly. A white-haired speaker, a great logistics specialist, said "outside the comfort zone" repeatedly until he was no longer the affable Dickensian gentleman whose presence was enjoyed on many a stage. A well-known CEO regularly plunks "thinking outside the box" into any sentence that'll usefully carry the phrase until you want to bite an ankle, particularly his. Then there's the Human Resources' specialist who says "etcetera, etcetera" when she can think of no other example with which to close a dreary sentence. There's also the American politician who always wants to ensure a "win-win situation" in every paragraph of any speech. And finally there's the detested "going forward," used by ninety percent of the speakers who have graced any meeting or any stage over the last two or three years. You don't need these things. And avoid clichés. Most clichés use metaphors, which are fine when the speaker has a sense of what he or she is doing with them but bad when the imagery of the expression is being used accidentally and without any real linguistic or useful appreciation.

Don't Get on Your Listeners' Nerves

Other ways of getting on your audience's collective nerves occur because of a lack of knowledge. This includes knowledge of your audience demographics. But other, perhaps more mundane aspects are important. Proper dress is key. Yes, there are presenters who can arrive on stage on a motorcycle dressed in leather. And, yes, you can get away with jeans and a T-shirt proclaiming your love of the band Motorhead. And you can wear another pair of jeans and open-toe sandals if you're Steve Jobs. But whatever your taste, do the courteous thing and ask the organizers what the audience members will be wearing, and once you have the answer, be considerate. Not stuffy, just considerate. And consider how you want to be seen. Refrain from wearing very bright clothing, sparkling jewelry, and clanging bracelets. (And that's just the gentlemen.)

Another thing that really irritates audiences is a presenter or speaker who paces rapidly back and forth on stage. This makes your audience dizzy or uncomfortable and distracts from your message. Plan your moves to emphasize your points and to include your entire audience. If more people took notice of this one piece of advice, then very good speakers might become close to great. It's easy to get carried away (literally). There was the professor of social science who became so engrossed in his explanation of something that he paced up and down the stage and occasionally waved at the PowerPoint on the very large screen behind him. At one point, in a paroxysm of absolute excitement, he went to touch a bullet point—totally forgetting that the screen wasn't solid and that there was a drop of five feet behind the stage edge where the screen stopped. He teetered, and the crowd held its by now exhausted breath, secretly praying for a bit of afternoon excitement. The good professor tried to grab the screen. The screen sagged and bent like a sail on a raft in an Atlantic squall. The professor, already running forty minutes over, all but disappeared. Luckily, the gods were smiling upon him (well, it was in Athens), although why they were nobody could guess, and he stopped himself from toppling into the abyss. What's quite extraordinary is that he barely missed a beat and went on for another thirty minutes during which time everyone now desperately wanted him to repeat the trick and disappear for good.

Don't adopt strange stances, like the otherwise likeable marketing director who thrusts his hands deep into his trouser pockets and plays with his loose change. While there, he decides to adjust his underwear and other bits and pieces. Not a good look. Neither is it visually satisfying to see strange shoes, weird socks (although odd socks have some charm), tomato soup on a shirt, pants undone or a skirt that doesn't fold with ease as a lady sits. Squeaking shoes and clanking jewelry don't have much attraction either. In terms of movement, use the entire stage and make a point of moving around it with purpose. Don't wring your hands either. It looks pathetic, creates the impression that you're pleading with kidknappers and shows no confidence. In fact it makes your audience nervous. Use your hands to make appropriate gestures and leave them at your sides when not gesturing. Be natural. If you feel like it, hold a pen in one hand; it helps.

Start Strongly

Some of the top executives or politicians in the world step up to the platform and fall flat on their faces as speakers. How could these intelligent, business-savvy executives, who are so adept at running a company, end up boring an audience? How can they want the tumbleweed to tumble and the dry wind to whistle through the auditorium so early in the performance? Many speakers begin with a polite, "Thank you very much for that kind introduction." Rather trite, don't you think? Instead, start with a bang not a whimper. Give them a startling statistic, an "in your face" statement, an interesting quote, a news headline, a powerful something, that will get your listeners' attention immediately. The last time someone read to you the "someone" was probably your mother and she was trying to get you to sleep. So, lesson learned, instead of reading your speech verbatim, use a keyword outline. These keywords will prompt complete thoughts as you speak. Look down at the keyword, look into the eyes of the audience—then talk. Honestly, it's easier than you might believe. Also, your audience wants to connect with *you*. Your audience will connect with you when you tell your own stories, not stories that people will know you pinched from *Chicken Soup for the Soul* by Jack Canfield and Mark Victor Hansen (1993) or age-old, unoriginal tales about Winston Churchill's comments at dinner parties. While you might (and sometimes absolutely must) weave in brief quotes or short stories from other sources, you should sometimes illustrate your most profound thoughts from your own actual life experiences. And if you don't think you have any interesting personal stories to tell, you aren't looking deeply enough. Look harder.

POINTS TO REMEMBER

- Your job as a speaker is to get a strong reaction—in your favor of course. Be very clear about what reaction you want.
- Consider why you want the audience to agree with you. Think about how people can benefit from what you have to say.
- Don't just repeat the same speech time after time. Why do you imagine that every audience is the same?
- Connect with your audiences. Explain why your topic is important. It's your job to engage those in your audience. Ensure that what you have to say is relevant. Put yourself in their position. What would you think of you?
- Inspire your audiences. It really is your job to get people to believe in what you have to say. Be interesting, innovative, challenging, and exciting. That takes work—each and every time.
- Be aware of how you behave on stage, and how you move and use the space.
- Always begin strongly.

Chapter Nine
Jargon and Other Rubbish

"Generally, when people use jargon not to communicate but to impress their audiences with their importance...or use it to announce membership in a group, communication suffers and the jargon can quickly degenerate into something close to the twittering of birds."
W. Lutz, "Jargon," *Oxford Companion to the English Language* (1992)

The esteemed drama critic and translator Eric Bentley said, "Ours is the age of substitutes: instead of language, we have jargon." You know that repeated and unnecessary words are an irritant that can become an audience's open wound. The same applies to jargon. Avoid it unless you're an expert talking to experts who understand the jargon code of your and their expertise. There are some who think that using buzzwords or subject terminology in speeches is a good idea. It is not. Many is the time that at banking conferences, there have been bankers listening to senior bankers, where it's plain as daylight that the majority of the audience genuinely don't understand "commodity super-cycle," "light-touch regulation," "tax equivalent yield," or even "share of wallet." Well, maybe not the last one. Yes, you're right, of course—shame on them and they should all be fired. But, like a lot of these scenarios, it's a case of the emperor's new clothes, where nobody dares say "Excuse me, senior vice president who dictates my bonuses and keeps me in gainful employment, but would you mind telling me what 'disintermediation' means?" Would you ask that? Well, for the curious among you, let's demystify "disintermediation." In an economy, the movement of savings or investment funds away from institutions such as banks into higher-yielding investments in the securities markets such as money market funds or bonds is called disintermediation. Let's pause for breath. Do you feel better now? Of course you don't—unless you're a disintermediation specialist, in which case you're looking around the departure lounge right now and smiling at everyone knowingly.

Never Assume that Your Audience Will Understand Jargon

There have been several occasions at large corporate events when financial experts have clearly understood phrases such as "deferred annuity" (as do you of course) but struggled visibly with something like "defensive stock," a phrase that a particular management consultant (guest speaker at considerable cost) repeated to the point where most in the audience were considering going to prison for a very long time for what they would have liked to have done to him. Again for those who care, "defensive stock" is a stock or share whose price remains stable or declines less in a falling market because demand for its product or service doesn't decline in a slowing economy. See? For example, the stocks of utilities and food businesses are "defensive" because people still use electricity and buy food in down markets, but we may defer the purchase of a new car. Anyway, the point is (relatively) clear and it's worth making again: don't try and be smart at the expense of your audience. You may be seen as an expert, but the best experts are not always the best communicators, and the best communicators don't try and baffle with jargon or an expression of complicated ideas that require long gestation. If your audience is trying hard to understand what you said five minutes ago, you've lost the plot and, more importantly, your audience. You have to be sure that your audience is traveling with you. That also means that you mustn't oversimplify and treat those in the audience like idiots or simpletons. It's a difficult balance, but one that is largely overcome by ensuring that you know as much as you possibly can about the people to whom you're speaking. Once again, the best advice is worth repeating. Know thy audience. If you do, then you'll know the style and language to use. You can't always get it a hundred percent right, but close is good and actually essential. Direct, straightforward language is always better than a plethora of acronyms and specialist dogma. If in doubt, don't.

Vocabulary

That brings us to the use of vocabulary. Again, choose vocabulary that you know that your audience will by and large understand. Here lessons can be learned (generally speaking) from experienced politicians and, in particular, prime ministers and presidents of countries and nation-states. They will normally use a middle range of words that they know pretty much all of their listeners will "get." Although there are notable exceptions when audiences listening to certain politicians (and business people) look as blank at the end of a speech as they did at the beginning. Or, worse, they think that what they heard was moderately encouraging and, as they leave, they nod wisely. Don't follow that path. Do your homework and establish what your audience members know. All the questions you need to ask are obvious. Suffice it to say that being precise in how you say what you say will mean that your audience will understand what you're talking about. That means that they will give you a fair hearing. It doesn't necessarily mean that they will agree or find what you say amusing, entertaining, or correct. The use of the right vocabulary is key for direct communication. For example, if you're going to expose unethical behavior of medical insurance companies, ensure that the word "unethical" recurs instead of switching to "immoral," "wrong," or "bad." Occasional, underline occasional, repetition of the same terms makes it easier for your audience to take in and connect information.

People hide behind inappropriate use of language. Avoid using euphemisms (words that veil the truth, such as "collateral damage" for the unintended destruction of civilians and their property) and other deceitful language. The following doesn't get said everyday but on enough days it does: "Look at these sales figures, everyone. You know, you can't put lipstick on a pig, despite what Sarah Palin says! If we continue this strategic virtual circle, we'll really cut the mustard and rise to the very top of the milk. The way going forward is clear and the long and winding road is not that hard. We must drive true north and ensure that our battle lines are drawn." When this type of nonsense is delivered very few of us challenge it. Why? Because we're afraid to give offense, or because we don't want to display ignorance, just in case the nonsense actually does mean something. The use of specialized terms, idioms, expressions, acronyms, and abbreviations that are understandable to only a select group of people (or actually none) is unfair to the rest of the people suffering in a warm auditorium on a sunny day with little prospect of much for lunch other than curled sandwiches. They will most likely "turn off" and cease listening or maybe even become antagonistic toward you or the ideas you are trying to present.

It is said that jargon has its function in the workplace. It is said that it can provide a useful shorthand to get across specific meaning quickly. Both assumptions are not true. The thing with business jargon is that it's in danger of being confusing at best and meaningless at worst. Nonetheless, it's rife. Government agencies are the perhaps the worst culprits. Such business-speak gems as "predictors of beaconicity" and "holistic governance" confuse or obscure meaning rather than clarify it. A dense phrase such as "across the piece" can be simplified to "everyone working together," and the pretentious word "actioned" can be replaced with the simple "do." Why do we have to have "coterminous stakeholder engagement" when we could just "talk to people" instead? You will be able to think of other examples. Of course, you may like jargon;

you may think it's valuable in all that you say and write. What a great dinner guest you must make. You will talk of new organizational paradigms, and you'll want to achieve alignment between learning and strategic priorities. And that's before the main course. Your fellow diners will have slipped numbed to the core under the table.

Most of us have pet hates when it comes to jargon. Many people find "thinking outside the box" and "blue-sky thinking" particularly annoying. Organizations "apply resources" (instead of putting people in roles or jobs); they "cascade" (communicate); and they even have a number of "strategic staircases" (plans for the future). And commentators at large who complain of jargon phrases used in office life, in corporate and political literature, and in speeches and presentations are sometimes at fault themselves. There is one British organization which castigated those who use "in the loop" and "re-baselining" but itself made use of "in the loop" on its own Web site with annoying regularity. So, is jargon now an acceptable form where, as in many other scenarios, we simply have to go with the flow? "No" is the direct answer. If something isn't clear in its meaning, then it should not be used, and we must stop this application of the emperor's new clothes where we are embarrassed or frightened to ask for clarity.

Avoiding Jargon

There are other reasons to avoid jargon. Without question, the use of jargon masks uncertainty or ignorance. It's also used by people aiming to assert their superiority, and this is based upon the common misconception that we are to blame when we don't understand something. It's our fault apparently that we don't understand the communicator, and therefore we're made to feel guilty or uncomfortable. The use of jargon can also be a way of trying to show exclusivity, encouraging the concept that only those who understand the language are "in the club." Some in industry, including Jack Welch of GE fame, Greg Dyke former Director General of the BBC, and Steve Jobs, and some presidents have managed relatively jargon-free organizations. But even in communication businesses like advertising agencies, jargon is unfortunately all too common and ingrained. Woe betide you if you join Sally Shoesmith's advertising agency on a Monday and by lunchtime on that day you haven't got up to speed with the lingo.

Some healthy organizations identify the words and phrases that are most overused and irritate or confuse people. Management then bans their use. Other organizations go one step further—utilizing e-mail and Web-filtering technology to flag or block the words they've banned. PricewaterhouseCoopers has spent time and money educating its board to "de-jargonize," encouraging individuals to hold each other to account if they slip. Jargon-speak is particularly confusing where businesses operate over more than one country, and where those whose first language is different from that of other staff find the jargon impossible to understand or, worse, to interpret. And so it is with people who aspire to greatness in speechmaking. Try not to use jargon even if you believe that your audience will understand every acronym or buzz phrase. Undoubtedly and undeniably there will be some in the audience whom you will lose. There are those who believe that jargon will speed up communication, that it creates a shared purpose and ensures that everyone knows what is expected of them. But it's not really a valid shorthand, and it flatters no one and assists little. Take a look at these clichéd phrases (and meanings), and try to avoid using them or any like them:

- cross-fertilization = the spreading and sharing of ideas
- income streams = money from a variety of products, initiatives, or services
- low-hanging fruit = a quick win or an easy success
- 360-degree thinking = taking everything or all arguments into consideration

- singing from the same hymn (or song) sheet = thinking similarly
- to get all our ducks in a row = to get organized
- helicopter view = overview
- to think outside the box = to think differently
- to fast-track = to speed up (or it can mean a quick route to a top position)
- to look under the hood = to analyze
- blue-sky thinking = shaping random ideas

Eventually, employees use jargon and company vocabulary without thinking, even if they don't know quite what is meant by the word or phrase. That being the case, its use becomes obstructive and irritating. Or it takes on a new meaning. Overall, jargon is more common around the world in larger organizations than smaller ones. At a recent conference on "human capital," a senior Australian specialist in "people management for small companies" was asked a question. She replied that she could not be totally accurate because she didn't have the "bandwidth" to deal with the issue. The (up until that point) good nature of the event disappeared in a puff of smoke, and there descended a silence. Tumbleweed did indeed tumble. At the same event the next day another speaker was talking about a new Human Resources process that was not yet sufficiently "big-banged" in his company. He meant "launched," but most people in the audience didn't understand that, and, once more, you could see the tumbleweed and hear the whistle of the wind.

Management-speak

Management-speak can be dangerous (and enormously dull), and it's not just a British or an American problem. Conferences, events, political rallies, universities, schools, and even weddings in all parts of the world find on occasion a plethora of politicians, business speakers, tutors, teachers, and proud fathers who use (or hide behind) jargon. One employer recently commanded that staff should not use the word "brainstorm" for a discussion. The reason posited was that the connotations were negative and might be associated with fits! The phrase that employees were asked to use instead was "idea showers." Anyone involved with a particular product at an American multinational business was encouraged to be a "product evangelist." And software users these days, so we hear, want to be "platform atheists" so that their computers will run programs from any manufacturer. In recent years friends have been asked to "touch base about something—offline," which just means "let's have a private conversation." A very senior director of an international bank had several terrific examples in his keynote presentation opening: "We need a holistic, cradle-to-grave approach," "You are all on my radar," "Let's pre-plan and then pre-plan some more," and "How can we help our customers in this space going forward?" An eminent guest speaker at a large and prestigious Nebraska conference said, as part of his closing remarks, that "I will give this my full support from the get-go" and "You will need to get all your ducks in a row now—before the five-year-olds wake up." As some might say, "go figure."

And Political-speak

Politicians are not exempt. An Australian politician recently commented in a speech that he would "get his fingers down the throat of the organization of that nodule." He concluded that "we must press on and of course my door is open on this issue and at the end of the day, at the close of play, we will clarify the detail. We need to check where we're at and move forward at 110 per cent." Then there's the great comment from an event in Dubai that "we too used to have daily paradigm shifts, but now we have stakeholders who must come to the party or be left out, or whatever." A famous politician was presenting to a pharmaceutical division of a multinational; she referred to the operation as "a really cool train set." That was sort of OK, and one could let that go because it was relatively sweet, but she also solemnly promised "to leverage the country's talents, to display unyielding integrity." Where would this happen she was asked? Why, she said, on the "strategic staircase." There's a device that's been around in various guises for a long time, something often called the Buzz Phrase Generator. Basically, it's a series of three columns of words, and you can choose at random one word from each column to make yourself a sudden expert on anything. So you end up with phrases like "overall digital programming" or "compatible third-generation hardware" or "parallel monitored mobility." This is instant expertise, and the scary thing is that many would nod wisely and agree with you when you spout this stuff. Jargon becomes a problem when it stops people understanding your message. That's the problem. Jargon diminishes the effectiveness of the communication.

POINTS TO REMEMBER

- Use vocabulary suitable for your audience. It's all about you helping your audience to understand your proposition. There is no value in creating barriers.
- Avoid using euphemisms (the substitution of an unpleasant or offending word or phrase by one that is less offensive). Examples: pre-owned for second-hand, between jobs for unemployed, economical with the truth for lying.
- If something isn't clear in its meaning then it shouldn't be used.
- People sometimes use jargon as a way of trying to show exclusivity. Avoid this. It's unnecessary. It doesn't make you look or sound smarter. Don't show off.
- If people in your audience have to work too hard to understand anything you're saying they will give up and switch off.

- Once again, know your audience. If you do, you'll know better how to pitch your speech.
- An acronym or two may be used but do try to avoid them. They're confusing. An acronym is a word formed from the initial letters of an idea, name or organization. Examples: NATO for North Atlantic Treaty Organization, KISS for Keep It Simple Stupid, CALL for Computer Assisted Language Learning, and NIMBY for Not In My Back Yard.

Chapter Ten
Persuasion

> "I would rather try to persuade a man to go along,
> because once I have persuaded him, he will stick. If I
> scare him, he will stay just as long as he is scared,
> and then he is gone."
> Dwight D. Eisenhower (1890–1969)

Aristotle was very clear about what persuasion meant. His first principle of persuasion as posited in *Rhetoric* (367–347 B.C.) was "to well dispose your audience to you and ill dispose them to your enemy." David Ogilvy, that great name of advertising, wrote in *Ogilvy on Advertising* (1983), "I don't know the rules of grammar. If you're trying to persuade people to do something, or buy something, it seems to me you should use their language..." Similarly, Benjamin Franklin was convinced that if, as a speaker, you wanted to persuade your audience then you had to focus on their interests. There's nothing wrong with persuasion. The word has had foisted upon it all kinds of strange and dark meanings, but here we are merely ascribing to it the action of inducing someone to believe in something. Over the ages, there have developed a number of methods by which people can persuade audience members in speeches. These methods can ensure that an argument sounds good or that it might reinforce a listener's thinking. Emotion plays a part too.

Persuasion and Argument
Antithesis (a figure of speech in which sharply contrasting ideas are juxtaposed in a balanced or parallel phrase) is a brilliant device for

speeches. It's the use of two contrasting words, phrases, or sentences placed directly opposite one another. Antithesis uses the contrast principle to draw attention to something. When an opposite to what might be expected is given, it is usually a surprise and hence causes the listener to slow down and consider the puzzle presented. Here's an example from the German writer Goethe: "Love is an ideal thing, marriage a real thing." Another comes from a 1964 St Louis speech given by Martin Luther King Jr., "We must learn to live together as brothers or perish together as fools." "To err is human, to forgive, divine," is an example from the poet Alexander Pope. Essentially antithesis is a group of words and phrases with opposite meanings balanced against each other. Barack Obama of course uses antithesis to great effect. From a Chicago speech comes: "If we are going to make the investments we need, we also have to be willing to shed the spending that we don't need," and "In these challenging times, when we're facing both rising deficits and a sinking economy, budget reform is not an option. It's a necessity." Barry Goldwater, Republican candidate for the presidency said in 1964, "Extremism in defense of liberty is no vice, moderation in the pursuit of justice is no virtue." William Shakespeare had Brutus in the play *Julius Caesar* say, "Not that I loved Caesar less, but that I loved Rome more."

John F. Kennedy enjoyed both antithesis and triads. This is from Kennedy's inaugural speech opening: "We observe today not a victory of party, but a celebration of freedom—symbolizing an end, as well as a beginning—signifying renewal, as well as change." Here's Hillary Clinton: "Government must be about 'We the people' not 'We the favored few.'" John McCain: "I will keep taxes low and cut them where I can. My opponent will raise them." This is cleverly a double antithesis: "I" versus "My opponent" and "keep taxes low" against "raise them." There are a myriad of examples from the world of politics, but fewer from business. So, if you're in business, try the device. It's powerful and effective.

Try your own examples of antithesis. Relate a couple to your own life or work. Jot a few down now. One of the more famous examples is: "One small step for a man, one giant leap for all mankind." And there's the equally well-known: "The brave men, living and dead" from Lincoln's Gettysburg Address. You can assuredly see how this works now, and it's a very useful way to support an argument or reinforce one. It's a very persuasive device, and this is of course the point. Use whatever it takes to persuade an audience of your proposition. Antithesis is perfect. The principle of antithesis may also be used more broadly, for example, where a character in a play acts in contrary ways, or where two characters have diametrically opposite positions, thereby highlighting each other. Sometimes, you can use antithesis in a story, again, to make a point clear. A simple example is that of Snow White and the wicked witch from the fairy tale *Snow White and the Seven Dwarfs*. Snow White is the antithesis of her stepmother, the wicked witch. She is good, modest, innocent, kind, cheerful, and generous while the wicked witch is evil, vain, jealous, cruel, corrupt, crafty, miserable, and generally plain nasty.

The Rule of Three or Triad

One of the most common and effective rhetorical devices, as you now know, is called the rule of three, or a triad. When using the rule of three, you include three equal elements in a sentence or series of sentences. Here are a few examples: Abraham Lincoln's "government of the people, by the people, for the people, shall not perish from the earth," and Franklin D. Roosevelt's "I see one-third of a nation ill-housed, ill-clad, ill-nourished." Many people make the mistake of thinking repetition is simply another term for the rule of three. But repetition is not needed, as in this example from the American Declaration of Independence: "Life, liberty and the pursuit of happiness."

So why would you want to create a triad? Using a triad is an extraordinarily powerful way of emphasizing a persuasive point. It allows you to express concepts more completely, emphasize your points, and increase the power of your message—and that's why you're making your speech of course. Also, there are certain elements of speech that are easy on the ear in any language, and three is a number of items not difficult to assimilate. We tend to remember words and phrases more readily when they are packaged in threes. Lawyers and those giving sermons use the device to make a point, knowing full well that a jury or parishioners will readily recollect a list of three.

It's worth reinforcing the fact that the rule of three is a powerful speechwriting technique that you can easily master. Excellent examples abound in all cultures and in many disciplines. Some that come to mind include, "The truth, the whole truth, and nothing but the truth," "Father, Son, and Holy Ghost," "gold, frankincense, and myrrh," and the movie title *The Good, the Bad and the Ugly*. The French national motto, *Liberté, Égalité, Fraternité*, works, as does Shakespeare's "Friends, Romans, Countrymen. Lend me your ears," from *Julius Caesar*. Another example from Lincoln's Gettysburg Address is "We can not dedicate—we can not consecrate—we can not hallow—this ground." And another of Churchill's is a perennial favorite. It's a list of three combined with antithesis: "Never in the field of human conflict has so much been owed by so many to so few."

Rhetorical Magic

So, as you can begin to see, adding a touch of rhetorical magic is relatively easy in the construction of a speech. Throughout history all great speakers have used such devices to marvelous and powerful effect. Whatever it takes to persuade, to make your point clear and memorable must be worth considering. There is something special and satisfying about the rule of three. It allows you to make a point, emphasize it, and make it last. The rule of three describes triads of all types—any collection of three related elements. Two more specific triad variants are hendiatris (from the Greek: "one through three") and tricolon (a sentence with three clearly defined parts of equal length, usually independent clauses and of increasing strength). A hendiatris is a figure of speech where three successive words are used to express a central idea. Julius Caesar's "Veni, vidi, vici" is one of these and so too is "Wine, women, and song." In a strict tricolon, the elements have the same length, but this condition is often put aside. Examples of a tricolon would include Franklin D. Roosevelt's advice for orators: "Be sincere, be brief, be seated," or this from Obama's keynote speech to the Democratic National Convention in July 2004: "Tonight, we gather to affirm the greatness of our nation—not because of the height of our skyscrapers or the power of our military or the size of our economy." Here's another tricolon from Obama, this time from his inaugural speech: "Homes have been lost, jobs shed, businesses shuttered."

Whatever the reason, we find something complete and satisfying in a group of three. The use of triads is a traditional speechwriting technique, and actually you can get even more power out of a triad by carefully choosing the order and adding a twist to the last. And don't forget that the third element in a list of three is often followed by a pause when making a speech, so it will remain longer in your listeners' memories. Getting your audience to think deeper is important. You're there on stage. You have one chance of hitting home your message to Sally Shoesmith, to get your idea across to her and your colleagues and to explain your reasons for the fall in sales. The added element of humor in a triad is a useful trick as well, but as is the case with all jokes and funnies, be cautious. Consider one popular example that is attributed to both Benjamin Disraeli and Mark Twain: "There are three kinds of lies: lies, damned lies, and statistics." In a speech, that'd get a smile, possibly a laugh. The first two elements ("lies" and "damned lies") set a pattern in the mind of the audience. They expect a third element such as "white lies," "dreadful lies," or "the worst lies." The mismatch between expectation and reality can create humor, and humor can help cement your relationship with an audience; it can also lighten a mood and, at the same time, underline a serious point. The pattern distracts and therefore magnifies the surprise. Experienced speechmakers set a pattern and then break that pattern with a surprise, frequently and to great effect. Stand-up comedians do it all the time. The first sentence of a gag introduces a new topic. The second sentence establishes the pattern. The third sentence breaks the pattern with a punch line. Maximize *your* audience response by making the third element as weird or absurd as you can, while ensuring there is still a connection.

Alliteration

Alliteration is another useful speech tool. This is the repetition of consonant sounds in neighboring words or syllables, and it can work to reinforce or underline a major fact in your speech. It can be used in a triad or not—whatever works for you. One of the most famous lines Martin Luther King Jr. ever spoke was: "I have a dream...that my four little children will one day live in a nation where they will not be judged by the color of their skin but by the content of their character." Hear how the sound of the crisp "c" punctuates the sentence. Similarly, and from the same speech: "Five score years ago, a great American, in whose symbolic shadow we stand today..." Repetition of the same sound at the beginning of a word, such as the repetition of the "b" sounds in "beaded bubbles winking at the brim," from John Keats's *Ode to a Nightingale*, makes the language poetic and, once again, very comfortable on the ear. It helps listeners to remember. It sounds good. Coleridge used it well in the poem *Kubla Khan*: "Five miles meandering in a mazy motion." Apart from ease of language on the ear, a common use for alliteration is emphasis. It occurs in everyday speech in such phrases as "tittle-tattle," "bag and baggage," "bed and board," "through thick and thin," and "look before you leap." Again, this is all part of your armory of persuasion. People need to remember to be persuaded. They need to enjoy the lilt and rhythm of what they hear. You have enormous power if you use language and words well. By the way, be careful with alliteration. What looks good when written down can sound dreadful or, more likely, might cause you to stumble and then the moment's gone, your cool is lost and you sound foolish.

The Rhetorical Question

There are of course a plethora of devices that can be used, but we're specifically looking at persuasive methodology here. There are other tools that work well in constructing a powerful message. For example, there's the rhetorical question such as: "Can we really expect the country to keep paying for health care from its now limited resources?" The rhetorical question is usually defined as any question asked for a purpose other than to obtain the information the question asks. For example, "Why are you so stupid?" is likely to be a statement regarding one's opinion of the person addressed rather than a genuine request to know the answer. Apart from these more obviously rhetorical uses, the question as a grammatical form has important rhetorical uses. For example, a rhetorical question might be used as a method of beginning a conversation: "Shall I compare thee to a summer's day?" asks Shakespeare's 18th sonnet. This kind of question, in which one asks the opinion of those listening, is called anacoenosis (from the Greek meaning "to communicate" or "impart"). This rhetorical question has a definite ethical side, since to ask one generally endears the speaker to his or her audience and so improves his or her credibility (or ethos). It's a gentle form of questioning. Sometimes, a rhetorical question is asked only in a thought-provoking way to prompt debate, particularly a political one. For example, "How corrupt is the government?" is more or less a rhetorical question. This kind of question doesn't really have a concrete or absolute answer; the answer is opinion-based. A rhetorical question often includes a rhetorical expression or figure of speech as well. Sometimes, such an expression becomes a figure of speech over time. "Are you kidding?" is an example. When that happens, the phrase is no longer really a question at all.

Rhetorical questions are good attention-getting devices and can enhance a speech. This sort of thing works: "How lucky are we to be here on this sunny day at this great event?" But many speakers make the mistake of opening their speech with rhetorical questions as a means to grab attention right away. This isn't always the best idea because the most awkward part of a speech for both the speaker and the audience is usually the first few moments. In most cases, the speaker hasn't yet established rapport with the audience. If rapport hasn't been established yet, the audience can be confused about how to react to the rhetorical question. The audience might be thinking, "Is he or she expecting an answer?" or "Shall I shout out? Will anyone else shout out?" Or, "Am I supposed to do something or react?" Or "Oh my goodness, this presentation is going to be interactive. Hide!" This is compounded by the fact that many speakers *do* actually want an answer and therefore spend the first five minutes asking people in the front row a question that everyone thought was rhetorical. The fact that nobody, including the speaker, can hear any of the answers only digs the hole deeper. So the question rhetorical is useful but needs handling with some caution. Otherwise distraction can ensue as fast as engagement can disappear.

Other Forms of Questioning

There are other types of questioning that can work for you. Hypophora (from the Greek "rebuke" or "reply") consists of raising one or more questions and then proceeding to answer them yourself, usually at some length and immediately—a big difference from the rhetorical. A common method is to posit the question at the beginning of a speech section and then use that section to answer it: "What can we do about nuclear proliferation in the Middle East? My theory is this..." Or, "How can we be decisive about Shakespeare's life with the little we know? Well, the documents that we have to hand do indicate..." This is an attractive device because asking an appropriate question appears quite normal and helps to maintain audience curiosity and interest. The audience members also know that they're not expected to answer. You can use hypophora to raise questions that you think the listener obviously has on his or her mind and would like to see formulated and answered by you: "But what will the result of this strategy be on staff numbers? The new product sales clearly indicate..." Some speakers use this methodology to take the carpet from right underneath the listeners' feet on the basis that they (the speakers) know full well what issues are uppermost in the audience's collective mind. It's also a useful device when addressing a small group—like Sally Shoesmith's. And hypophora can be used as a transitional or guiding device to change directions or enter a new area of discussion: "But what are the implications of this theory? And how can it be applied to the present difficulty of sales?" A group of questions set up to be answered precisely and accurately can keep a speech lively and interesting.

Anaphora

Anaphora (from the Greek, meaning "carrying back") is another useful device in persuasion. An anaphora is where the same word or phrase is used to begin successive clauses or sentences so the listener's attention is drawn directly to the message of the sentence. Here's an example from Raymond Chandler's *Farewell My Lovely* (1940): "I needed a drink, I needed a lot of life insurance, I needed a vacation, I needed a home in the country. What I had was a coat, a hat and a gun." And here's another example, this one from Winston Churchill's speech to the House of Commons on June 4, 1940: "We shall go on to the end, we shall fight in France, we shall fight on the seas and oceans, we shall fight with growing confidence and growing strength in the air, we shall defend our Island, whatever the cost may be, we shall fight on the beaches, we shall fight on the landing grounds, we shall fight in the fields and in the streets, we shall fight in the hills; we shall never surrender." Anaphora is often used in conjunction with parallelism (similarity of structure in a pair or series of related words, phrases, or clauses) or climax (an arrangement of clauses in ascending order of forcefulness). There's an example in Kinky Friedman's book *When the Cat's Away* (1988): "I'm not afraid to die...I'm not afraid to live. I'm not afraid to fail. I'm not afraid to succeed. I'm not afraid to fall in love. I'm not afraid to be alone. I'm just afraid I might have to stop talking about myself for five minutes." And one from Obama's book *The Audacity of Hope* (2004): "It's the hope of slaves sitting around a fire singing freedom songs; the hope of immigrants setting out for distant shores; the hope of a young naval lieutenant bravely patrolling the Mekong Delta; the hope of a millworker's son who dares to defy the odds; the hope of a skinny kid with a funny name who believes that America has a place for him, too." You can emulate all of this and it can be powerful and heady stuff in any speech.

Parallelisms

Parallelisms raised their cheery heads just now. Used well, they too can add persuasive value to a great speech. A parallelism is one of the most useful and flexible rhetorical techniques. It refers to any structure that brings together parallel elements, be these nouns, adjectives, verbs, or adverbs. A parallelism can be employed in many different ways. One application is inversion or chiasmus (from the Greek meaning "to shape like the letter X"), in which parallel elements are carefully reversed for emphasis. A famous example comes from President John F. Kennedy's inaugural address (1961): "Ask not what your country can do for you—ask what you can do for your country." Inversion often gains power by focusing attention on the ends of sentences, where readers and listeners naturally pause. Kennedy's example shows this, which is one reason why it's quoted so frequently. Constructed and delivered well, parallelism imparts grace and power to a speech. This example is from the nineteenth-century English essayist William Hazlitt: "The more we do, the more we can do." Woody Allen, a great writer of the quick New York wit: "I don't want to live on in my work. I want to live on in my apartment." And here's Jesse Jackson: "Today's students can put dope in their veins or hope in their brains. If they can conceive it and believe it, they can achieve it. They must know it is not their aptitude but their attitude that will determine their altitude."

Climax

Climax is an arrangement of words, phrases, or clauses in order of increasing importance, for example: "Ms Palin was more than eager to serve her family, her community and her nation." An example from Martin Luther King Jr.: "the unalienable rights of life, liberty and the pursuit of happiness." More specifically, climax is an increase in intensity brought about through the use of repeated words or phrases arranged by degrees of increasing significance, for example: "In the beginning was the Word, and the Word was with God, and the Word was God." (King James Bible, John 1:1–2). Another example from *Ulysses* by Alfred Lord Tennyson: "One equal temper of heroic hearts / Made weak by time and fate, but strong in will / To strive, to seek, to find, and not to yield." The use of climax is good in the creation of a powerful list describing an aspect of the point you're making. The device, like many others, allows for a form of verbal underlining.

The Art of Persuasion

The art of persuasive speaking was mastered by Roman and Greek orators such as Cicero and Demosthenes, who used multiple techniques to win over their audiences, in venues from law courts to public assemblies. They had no lights, no microphones, little in the way of props. Most rhetorical devices are still called by Greek and Latin names—but they endure in the speeches of modern politicians, including some of the most famous American presidents of recent memory. In 1952, Senator Richard Nixon, as he then was, gave his dramatic Checkers speech on television, successfully defusing a funding scandal that nearly lost him the vice-presidential nomination. Nixon, an astute lawyer, was adept at the kind of persuasion necessary in courtrooms. For instance, Nixon employed *occupatio* (Latin for "anticipation," and meaning seizing an opportunity to respond to your own point before anyone else can question it) a number of times in the speech: "But then some of you will say and rightly, 'Well, what did you use the fund for, Senator? Why did you have to have it?'" By bringing up likely objections to his own argument then answering them himself, Nixon framed the debate on his own terms. Nixon also used *praeteritio* (literally "passing over," in Latin), a more cynical trick of bringing up a controversial point by claiming to avoid it: "Incidentally, my opponent...does have his wife on the payroll... That's his business and I'm not critical of him for doing that. You will have to pass judgment on that particular point. But I have never done that." Nasty perhaps, but extraordinarily clever.

Classical oratory, then, is still used in recent times and even now. JFK's inaugural address from 1961 contains a number of flourishes common to classical oratory and frequently copied since. He employed hyperbole (exaggerated statements) when he declared, "Let every nation know, whether it wishes us well or ill, that we shall pay any price, bear any burden, meet any hardship, support any friend, oppose any foe, in order to assure the survival and the success of liberty." Kennedy's speech also demonstrated an elaborate construction called chiasmus. As we have already learned, this is Greek for "crossing." Chiasmus refers to the X shape of the Greek letter chi. It occurs when key words or ideas are arranged in an A-B-B-A pattern (*not* the pop group, no), for example when Kennedy observed that "For only when our arms are sufficiently beyond doubt can we be certain beyond doubt that they will never be employed." Another example, this time from Cormac McCarthy's *The Road* (2006), is: "You forget what you want to remember, and you remember what you want to forget." Yet another good example is from William Shakespeare's *Macbeth* (1i): "Fair is foul, and foul is fair." The magnificent Frederick Douglass in *An Appeal to Congress for Impartial Suffrage* (1867) said, "If black men have no rights in the eyes of the white men, of course the whites can have none in the eyes of the blacks." And here is an example from Barack Obama of course: "My job is not to represent Washington to you, but to represent you to Washington."

All great politicians and business executives of recent memory have been no strangers to the same rhetorical devices used in classical times. Clever argumentation, high-flown promises, and carefully constructed statements may have been used by them all, in particular Nixon, Kennedy, and Obama, but the devices are as old as the hills. Of course, there are more rhetorical devices than those here mentioned. Many others exist in classical oratory, and several can be found in the speeches of all those speakers who aim to speak like a president, sometimes because they are.

POINTS TO REMEMBER

- Devices from Greek and Roman oratory are still pertinent to speech structures today.
- The heart of any speech is the thesis, antithesis, and synthesis. The thesis is your core idea or argument, the antithesis is the opposite or contrast to your argument, and then the synthesis is the improvement of, or building on, your proposition to form a solid conclusion.
- The rule of three or triad involves including three equal elements in a sentence or series of sentences. A triad is a powerful way of reinforcing a point. It creates emphasis. We remember words or phrases more readily when put into threes.

- Alliteration is useful for reinforcing any important point in your speech.
- Rhetorical questioning is a great device for posing a question to prompt debate. You don't really expect an answer but it's a good way of getting attention for a particular point.
- Hypophora is good to use at the beginning of a speech or speech section. You ask a question and then your job is to use the rest of the speech or that speech section to answer it.
- Anaphora is where the same word or phrase is used to begin successive clauses or sentences so that your listeners' attention is drawn to the core message of that sentence.
- Parallelisms impart grace and power to a speech.
- Mark Twain thought that if a preacher couldn't save a sinner after twenty minutes, then the cause was lost. If you're going to persuade people through your oratory, don't wait until the end of your speech. Start at the beginning and get on with it.

Chapter Eleven
Structure?
What Structure?

"Speech is the twin of my vision, it is unequal to measure itself, it provokes me forever, it says sarcastically, Walt you contain enough, why don't you let it out then?"
Walt Whitman (1819-1892)

Speech structure is important along with everything else that's important about making a speech. Without structure you have no chance of succeeding in making that great speech at all. There are various schools of thought about structuring a speech, and there are equal numbers of views about how a speech should be written, some saying that it shouldn't be written at all. That view can't possibly ever work unless you have a photographic memory and simply know one or two set speeches inside out. Even then, one might argue that you couldn't possibly make one version fit all. The writing of a speech, its preparation on paper, is hard. Some executives and politicians employ speechwriters. Some use a team of writers much as often occurs with soaps, cartoons like *The Simpsons*, or any television comedy or drama. Good speech writing is rare. If you have a good writer working with or for you, nurture him or her. She or he is as scarce as gold dust.

Writing the Speech

But most of us have to write our own speeches. Perhaps you struggle in endless hours of speech preparation and still wind up with a speech that is unfocused, unclear, and with a meandering train of muddled thoughts. Well, there are a few easy fixes. Avoid the urge to start drafting your speech. Thrashing at a keyboard or scribbling endless thoughts with pen or pencil might be great exercise for your hands and creativity but might distract you from the objective of writing a good speech quickly. Some say that it's useful to write the conclusion first because that's what the audience remembers. The conclusion might be what the audience remembers best, but there's small value in this. What you really need to do is to write down the one main idea that you want the audience to hear, remember, and upon which to learn or act. That idea will also appear in the conclusion, of course. Without this one main idea or proposition you don't have a speech. It's the "this is what I'm talking about" moment. If the audience ignored everything else that you said or did, what one idea do you want the people in it to remember? One single sentence should do it. Remember, if this is hard for you, how do you think your audience is going to work it out? You want to impress, you want your speech to make an impact, and you want your message (that one line) to be remembered.

The proposition is driven in part by your expertise (otherwise why are you talking at all?) and by your audience's (hoped for) interest in that idea. Remember, once again, that you must know your audience—otherwise writing down your proposition will be ever difficult. But once you've established what the proposition is, you can begin to structure your speech. Start by identifying the points, stories, examples, or headings that support the proposition and make it come alive. These ideas must add to the argument supporting the proposition, not conflict with it (although you do need to know the opposing points so that later in the speech you can bring them up and defuse them—remember the point about taking the carpet from under the listeners' feet). Each of your supporting arguments should relate to the proposition and not stray off the main thesis. At this juncture, just make notes. In particular, consider how you might begin—the objective is to get the attention and interest of your audience, set the tone, reveal the topic, establish credibility, and get goodwill.

Be Organized

Then create headings and organize these into a sequence such as problem-cause-solution, step-by-step, they-me-you. A very good speech outline includes the past, present, and future. A common application of this is a persuasive speech where you offer up, say, a solution to a business problem. So first, you set the context by identifying a problem facing your company or division or department and describe how it came to be a problem in the first place (the past). Next, you lay out the decision to be made right now along with the alternatives from which to choose (the present). Finally, you paint a picture of positive outcomes—more income, better conditions, whatever—that will be realized if the right choice is made (the future), and perhaps you can use a successful case study or story to back up your premise. But you also need to show proof of success. Explain what it will look like and also say how everyone will know when they've got there. If you apply this sort of speech outline well, your audience will more readily understand your message. On the other hand, your audience is more likely to be confused if you repeatedly jump backward and forward in time (i.e., talk about the decision first, then the future prosperity, then the root cause of the past problem).

Another type of three-part speech outline for persuasive speeches involves complication, resolution, and example. In this case, begin your speech (introduction) by establishing the situation, problem, or opportunity, and then develop your case by setting out what is complicating, spoiling, or getting in the way of the likely success of whatever the situation is that you're describing. Next, show how what you say, if put into action, will absolutely solve the problem or create the opportunity. Finally, give the audience a clear example of how all this might work in practice, in their world. With your headings identified and sequenced, write the details that go under each heading. With a clear proposition and headings, writing the details is relatively straightforward, almost like filling in the blanks. Draw on your experiences or research anecdotes for relevant stories that will support each argument or point in support of the proposition. If you can, use stories that you already know, that you could tell to a colleague at a café or to your family at the dinner table. If you already know an anecdote or story, you don't have to bother writing it down; the first line or one word will do as a reminder. That will save a lot of time, and you can tell the same unwritten story hundreds of times, every time differently and every time perfectly. But be wary of telling the same story to the same audience. Corporate audiences (and political ones too for that matter) do get heartily fed up and not a little bored at the same routines from the same speakers. After you write the arguments or points in support of the proposition, make sure that the connections and links between each part of the speech work. Everything should support everything else. Keep it simple and logical.

Don't Forget the Power of Anecdotes

What stories or anecdotes will reinforce your case? Do they need to be adapted in any way to suit your audience? Consider what humor might work. How appropriate and what level? If in doubt, don't. Do you need to research a few quotes to support your proposition? Don't quote just for the sake of quoting—that will make you look foolish, not clever. Make any quote or illustrating example count. Also remember the rhetorical questions. Maybe you could begin with one or two? Or perhaps you could make a startling statement, for example: "In 2009, Americans spent $100.20 for every $100.00 they brought home." Or something like: "By 2020 there will be more people over the age of sixty in Germany than under twenty." Or: "Many have predicted the death of books in a digital age, but the fact is that more book titles are published today than ever, with increasing numbers sold online." Here are a few more ideas: "Killer whales, when traveling in groups, breathe in unison," "China has more English speakers than the United States," "Venus is the only planet that rotates clockwise," "You share your birthday with at least nine million other people in the world," "McDonald's restaurants serve food and drink to around 43 million customers a day," and "The first domain name ever registered was Symbolics.com in 1985." These are random ideas and you must seek out your own—based on your topic or theme. The point is that you should consider ways to arouse curiosity—perhaps a strange fact that will be explained, a prop the use of which will become clear, a magic trick involving an audience member, a striking piece of film, or a shocking piece of news. Avoid repeating the dreadful phrase "as I'll explain later" because most presenters never do. Refer to your audience regularly, relate to people's experiences; refer to current events or a previous speech or something with which the audience will be very familiar. These sorts of things always engage. Consider your visual support. Would a PowerPoint presentation work? If so, what kind and what format? If not PowerPoint, what else? Whatever you do use remember to keep it simple. What about video? OK, but keep it (or them) dynamic and short. Maybe you could show a startling or amusing TV commercial that helps make your point. Ask permission first or approach one of the many agencies that can get hold of these things for you at reasonably low cost. Don't show great chunks of your favorite movie on DVD. First, it's illegal, and second, *you* may enjoy ten minutes of Jabba the Hutt from one of the *Star Wars* movies but many in your audience might not.

As You Write, Always Consider the Audience

Create desire on the part of the audience to listen. Consider the kind of questions someone in the audience might ask, such as: "Why should I really care?" and "How does this topic relate to me at all?" Show the scope of the issue, the degree of importance and the ramifications of your proposition. That way you will engage the audience even if many in it don't always agree with you. Early on, reveal the topic and your interest or point of view. This is really important—people want to know where you stand and why. If times and dates are prevalent in your speech, keep them chronological—forward or backward. Remember, stick to your topic—don't stray. Don't use references that you consider may go over the heads of the audience, and don't be condescending. Remember, once again (it really is that important), the more you know about your audience the better. Be informative—a repeated and obvious point, one must suppose, but it's worth reminding you not to spend your time telling people what they already know.

Another important consideration when preparing your speech is to consider not just logic, but logical reasons why people should support your proposition. If your argument becomes irrefutable, you can't lose. But that doesn't mean you're right just because you say so—a point often forgotten by agitated politicians on TV. Of course, matters aren't usually so simple, and someone will always find a loophole in what you are arguing even if their loophole doesn't quite make sense. If the "loopholer" creates doubt, then others will possibly share that doubt and the hole gets bigger. Consider using a variety of support material for your case. Any facts, statistics (simple and direct), testimony (again simple and direct), and examples (yes, simple and direct) are all good to make your case watertight. Remember that all of this material must suit your particular audience. Make sure each point is developed completely (but not boringly) before going on to the next. And remember, too, that the more you know about the opposing view to your argument the better. Use that understanding to your advantage.

Transitions

Transitions are an important aspect of speechmaking. They are part of the process and connection of ideas. Think of sentences that will make it clear to the audience that you have finished one part of your argument and are now about to change pace or move to another. This is where devices like the rule of three can help you. The power of the number three is evident in many films, books, plays, moral tales, and children's stories that have a three-part structure, such as *Three Little Pigs* (the first two pigs get eaten up by the wolf because their houses were weak; the third pig's house of bricks was strong and so the wolf couldn't blow it down); *Goldilocks and the Three Bears*, in which one bowl of porridge was too hot, another was too cold, and the third bowl was just right; and the biblical story of the good Samaritan, which is another example of a three-act plot (the first and second travelers pass by, but the third, the Samaritan, helps an injured man who's been left at the side of the road). It's the same in movies: boy meets girl; boy loses girl; boy gets girl in the end. Or bad people hurt good people; good people rally with the help of a hero; bad people get beaten.

But it's not just children's stories and religious narratives that rely upon a neat three-act structure. Most stories, speeches, arguments, legal summations, and political commentary have three "acts." It is a generally held view that we are very comfortable with a simple three-act plot. And it's this comfort that can be leveraged by a skillful public speaker; your presentation gains warmth and familiarity. What you say at the start of a speech (and thereon) must of course arouse and then maintain audience interest in you and the subject; credibility must be gained and maintained and curiosity aroused. If you like (and only if it's appropriate), be provocative (without of course being rude or offensive) and, most definitely, break the audience's preoccupation with absolutely anything else that's going on inside the auditorium or any connection with any other topic or speaker or indeed the "outside world." Present the proposition clearly to, say, Ms Shoesmith's sales team: "I want to show you how sales for the next three months will fall, but I also want to show that the following three months after that will go through the roof." Arouse the audience's interest, and show how your proposition might or will be beneficial and met. Here you must encourage, inspire, motivate, call to action—all the things that you know need to be done. And said.

As You Prepare Your Speech, Remember Clarity

Connections within a speech are important, so that the whole moves seamlessly from one point to the next. This also aids clarity and that has to be an important factor in any speech. Use strong, straightforward transitions to help your listeners see how new information relates to what they've heard so far. If you set up a counterargument in one paragraph so you can demolish it in the next, begin the demolition by saying something like, "But this argument makes no sense when you consider that..." If you're providing additional information to support your main point, you could say, "Another fact that supports my main point is..." But you also have a role in helping your audience to listen. It's your job. A good device here is to rely on shorter, simpler sentence structures. Don't get too complicated when you're asking an audience to remember everything you say. Avoid using too many subordinate clauses, and place subjects and verbs close together. If your links are too complicated, then confusion reigns. For example, this doesn't work: "The new three-two-six-zero-slash-nineteen-zero-zero Mark 2, which was invented in 1929 by Sir Norbert Davenport-Smith in London, England, and which was on our store shelves around three years later, still sells amazingly well." But this does: "Sir Norbert Davenport-Smith invented the three-two-six series in 1929 and introduced it into stores shortly afterwards. Eighty years later, this extraordinary product still sells very well." It boils down to a simple fact. The more you read, the more easily will good sentence construction or ease of expression be at your disposal. The more you prepare a speech and rehearse it, the more likely are you to be better equipped to deliver it clearly. It doesn't happen by magic that someone has a good way with words or expresses him or herself well.

But there are ways to make the speaker's life easier. For example, pronoun use should be severely limited. Your listeners may have a hard time remembering or figuring out to what "it," "they," or "this" refers. Be specific by using a key noun instead of unclear pronouns. Look: "The British government has absolutely failed to protect its people from the plague of so-called reality television—that exploits sex, violence, and conflict and calls it human nature and is fine. This just can't continue to thrive." We don't understand "this." What is "this"? Is it the government's failure? Or is it reality TV or human nature? By the time you've thought it through, the speaker's moved on two paragraphs and you won't bother to play mental catch-up again. A better way of putting the sentence is: "The British government has failed to protect us from the plague of so-called reality television, which exploits sex, violence, and petty conflict and calls it human nature. This failure cannot continue." The proper phraseology requires some thought certainly, and if you find the prospect daunting then make life easier by making your sentences shorter. Whatever it takes to make your argument clear.

Keeping audience interest is key. Remember that one way of achieving that through your argument is to incorporate the rhetorical strategies of ethos, pathos, and logos. This, you will recall, is the Greek methodology of rhetoric and presenting an argument. When arguing a point, using ethos, pathos, and logos can help convince your audience to believe you and make your argument stronger. Ethos refers to an appeal to your audience by establishing your authenticity and trustworthiness as a speaker. If you employ pathos, you appeal to your audience's emotions—very important of course. Using logos includes the support of hard facts, statistics, and logical argument—an argument that builds a strong, irrefutable case. The most effective speeches usually present a combination of all three of these rhetorical strategies.

The most effective linking device is that of juxtaposing the main body of the speech to the close. Many times a speech that is otherwise good drifts off into the blue yonder, or it tapers out, because the speaker realizes that he or she is out of time, ideas, or connections, particularly as the end (or lunch) gets closer. The close is important. People will remember a good close in the same way that they'll forget a bad one. Speeches often close with an appeal to members of the audience to take action based on their new knowledge or understanding. If you do this, be sure that the action you recommend is specific, realistic, possible or achievable. For example, although your audience may not be able to affect foreign policy directly, they can vote or work for candidates whose foreign policy views they support. Relating the purpose of your speech to the lives of the people in your audience not only creates a connection with those people but also reiterates the importance of your topic to them.

Tell people exactly how you'll solve their problems—if that's your thesis. Be confident. Confidence (but, remember, not arrogance) implies that you're in control and that's something that you must always display on any stage. There's a reason why you're speaking in public. You're in control and have something important to say, even if it's explaining the rise or fall of the monthly sales figures in Sally Shoesmith's meeting. Making connections will help make your speech better than good. Structure forms connections. Greatness is won only by creating a structured speech with ideas connecting from start to finish. Greatness is an effort, and a great speech will make every link—every idea—clear, concise, and worthy of that effort.

POINTS TO REMEMBER

- When preparing for a speech, write down your core idea or proposition. This is what you want your listeners to remember.
- Write down everything in brief that supports your case and that makes your proposition work. What you say has to be

convincing, so you must ensure that your argument is fully supported. Something isn't necessarily right just because you say so.

- You will always need to know the opposing argument to yours. Build the opposing argument into your speech then take it apart. You don't need to do this in great detail but sufficient detail to ensure that people in your audience support your case.

- Consider your speech structure. A straightforward one is "past, present, and future." How this one works is that you tell your audience what things were like, then how things are now and finally how things will be or should be—according to you. You must always give examples of what you mean.

- Remember to use brief stories or anecdotes to highlight and support your points. Keep them relevant.

- Remember to research a few quotations to support your points. But don't quote just for the sake of it. Make your quotations relevant and appropriate. Don't just put in a quote because it sounds good. It has to mean something.

- Also remember that you can introduce rhetorical questions and some startling facts to reinforce your proposition and to attract attention. Arousing curiosity amongst your listeners is a good thing, but suggest nothing weird.

- Refer to current events or TV soaps. Mention current music or books. Show that you're up to speed with current affairs and the famous. All these things add value and currency to what you have to say. However, keep any example or reference relevant.

- A subordinate clause is part of a sentence; it contains a subject and verb but does not express a complete thought. These clauses can make sense on their own, but, they are dependent on the rest of the sentence for context and meaning. They are usually joined to an independent clause to form a complex sentence: "The door opened *because* the man pushed it." A subordinate clause which on its own does very little might be something like, "Because I was leaving." But adding a subordinate clause gives it sense: "Because I was leaving the waiter brought my overcoat." In speeches, there can be a tendency to have very complicated subordinate clauses—sometimes many in one sentence (or breath) and that doesn't help audience comprehension one bit.

Chapter Twelve
Body Languid

**"A blur of blinks, taps, jiggles, pivots and shifts...
the body language of a man wishing urgently to
be elsewhere."**
Edward R. Murrow (1908–1965)

A colleague was putting a president of a public company through
her paces the day before a very big conference where the said
president was due to address three thousand managers on the
merits of a merger very few wanted. After a couple of hours' rehearsal
the president, Brazilian, shook her head and said, "What I need now
is some good body language." Her assistant, who spoke very poor
English, ran to my colleague, the producer, and said hesitantly, "She
wants more body languid." Whether a president or not, each of us
gives off countless numbers of indications about our emotions and
frame of mind without even saying a word. Nonverbal communication
makes up a significant part of how we communicate with each other.
Different cultures and nationalities have their own body language
rules, as do different professions. Nonverbal communication and
especially body language communicate our thoughts and emotions
more than words. All of us are continually processing and giving off
nonverbal cues. Since body-language movements are made at a
subconscious level, they can often reveal things to others before a
conversation has even been started. These nonverbal cues are
picked up by the observer, who interprets them based on his or her
experience. This process is usually, but not always, two-way.

What Body Language Shows

The biggest contributor to body language of a strange kind is stage fright and nerves. Perhaps one of the biggest telltale signs of nervousness would be pacing and swaying movements on stage while you're speaking. When we're on stage we are sometimes understandably frightened or nervous, so we enter into the fight or flight mode. The adrenaline is pumping like mad, and suddenly the world seems to be unraveling in slow motion around us. Yikes. You've just developed the superhuman ability to speak in public, and you're not acutely aware of everything that's happening to you—your palpitating heart, your sweaty palms, and your shaking limbs. You can't keep still. And because you're still in your flight or fight mode, you're struggling to gain control of your feet. The result of this tension between the sharp desire to run and the obligation to stay and finish your presentation causes you to sway a little, and then you start to pace back and forth, to and fro. Though you don't even begin to realize it, this is not a good look. Similarly, there are those speakers who glue themselves to a lectern, grasping each side for dear life and keeping their heads down while reading their notes verbatim in a low mumble. Dare to look up, they think, and the gremlins will bite their legs. And then there's the CEO of a major bank who doesn't need notes (really he doesn't) and is confident. Knows his stuff. What does he do though? He thrusts his hands deep into his trouser pockets and plays with whatever's in there. Usually change. But, unsurprisingly, that's not a good and inspiring look either.

Making Body Language Work

So, what do you do? As you rehearse, work out and note down where and when you will make stage moves. Yes, it is a dull thing to have to do, and yes, we know you don't have time in your schedule. But, look, you're on stage. And like an actor you must prepare, you must know what you're going to do and where. Make all your moves look deliberate, and much of your nervousness will disappear. Standing still or moving with purpose puts you in total control. It's your speech, not the audience's. You're in charge.

What can be said about the language of famous bodies? Well, look at John McCain, for example. From his physical problems as a result of war wounds and torture, he is much more rigid than most and can't raise his arms easily. Unfortunately, that gives off a negative and less expressive look. He used his arms far less than Obama did or does. McCain looked conservative and staid. Along with his voice, McCain demonstrated management and safety, whereas Obama conveyed dynamic change. Body movement analysts say that McCain represented stability in how he stood firmly and held onto the sides of a lectern, leaning forwards slightly. An earnest, trustworthy look they said. He didn't grip the lectern for dear life but maintained a positive stance, of order. By contrast, Obama always has a forward-looking gaze and moves in a relaxed fashion during public appearances. John McCain sometimes adopted a right-left style of walking where he shifted his weight a little bit like John Wayne—a cowboy swagger, if taken to extremes. This could be of course out of necessity, given the man's past injuries. But that contrasts with Obama's more centered movement, where he manages his body in a relaxed and comfortable way. He makes sure that viewers see that he's comfortable, and he makes his stage companions or other members of state comfortable. Notice, for example, how he will often place a hand on the lower back or shoulder of the person with whom he's walking. It's not condescending but shows power and comfort. It makes us feel that he's in charge.

All business executives and politicians manage to break some rules around body language. For example, crossing arms while standing is regarded as defensive usually implying that you either want the questioning or difficult situation to stop or that you are very uncomfortable. Body language for actors is a vital part of their craft and really it's no less true for any speaker on any stage. In training, an actor is taught how to express emotion with his or her body, not just the face. It's possible for a very good actor to have his or her back to the audience and express very clearly a wide variety of emotions. Think about this. For a period of time you want members of your audience, Ms Shoesmith's twelve or a television audience of twelve million, to focus on you. The more you are aware of what you do on stage with face, arms, legs, and stance the more you will consider how to use body language to your advantage. The thing is not to think about it too much otherwise you will appear awkward, but do be sufficiently aware to notice if you do things which are seen as odd or distracting. Ask someone who's seen you present. On the whole, when you are presenting, stand proud with your stomach in, chest out, head up and look the audience in the eyes. This will make you feel more confident, and you will come over more confidently as well. The main thing to remember is that little things tend to irritate. So, try to avoid small repetitive movements.

Posture is important. Don't slouch. Practice standing straight. President Obama exhibits strength by his posture and the positioning of his chin. Look for this the next time you see him on TV. His head is always held high, with the chin slightly elevated. Remember, we all automatically lift our chins when we're proud; when we see someone with his or her chin elevated slightly, we subconsciously think of that person as more noble, strong, and trustworthy. Obama also smiles as though he knows that people at home like him. You smile too. The combination of the smile and the elevated chin is quite powerful. What's the effect on audiences? People tend to see Obama as positive, strong, and caring. This makes him worth listening to. He has credibility. Obama has become the master of cool and people like that—for the moment anyway. He clearly believes that how you say something is every bit as important as what is said and is equally as important as how you look while you're saying it. Why? This is because if you don't deliver the message in a compelling or credible manner it won't be absorbed. And if you don't look as if you believe that it's compelling, it won't be believed.

It's a generally held precept that anywhere in the world, nonverbal expression can show sadness, happiness, anger, fear, surprise, disgust, and contempt. It's quite easy to see how these facial expressions can flicker across someone's face in a fraction of a second, perhaps exposing their "true" emotions. Such micro-expressions can be seen regularly during TV interviews, and you need to try hard to avoid showing anger or surprise if these emotions don't suit your argument during a stage Q&A or a tough question from the floor or because someone's talking to his or her neighbor while you're in full flow. Show too much of the "wrong" expression at the wrong time and your argument (and much of your credibility) can disappear out of the air-conditioning vent. Since public figures often wear a public "mask" in order to gain social acceptability, such flickers of anger, amusement, or whatever can prove very interesting. When making judgments, we all rely more on what we see than solely on what we hear. Most people are simply not used to relying upon vocal cues only. How often are emotions misinterpreted over the telephone? Is intuition really a finely tuned sense of nonverbal cues, as some contend it often is? How many people don't pay attention to body language or facial expressions or discount what they do observe? Whatever we do on stage must be done for the benefit of our communication with the audience, including nonverbal cues.

Pauses

Pause like a president. Allow yourself and your audience a little time to reflect and think. Don't race through your presentation and leave your audience, as well as yourself, feeling out of breath. Obama's voice has always been rhythmic and hypnotic, much as a preacher's addressing his congregation. His voice is not unlike that of Martin Luther King (who of course was a preacher). King paused frequently to allow his crowds to assimilate, react or cheer. So too does Obama. So did American nineteenth-century preachers like Henry Ward Beecher and William Ellery Channing. Pausing is a way to control the audience. It's a powerful and dramatic tool that you can use to show dominance and strength. A pause slows down the pace and allows for reflection. The person pausing lacks any fear of being cut off by those surrounding him or her. An occasional short pause, lasting from one to three seconds, serves to separate the points you are making. All you have to remember is to slow down. Give the audience an opportunity to absorb what you are saying. Another effective pause is when you want to pretend to search for the best word or phrase. You may also think of using this kind of pause before any phrase or word you want to emphasize. Pauses of more than a couple of seconds can work well too. They can force the audience to think about what you just said. Such a pause brings with it weight. It's a tough thing to do, pausing. It's tough because you'll worry that the audience will sense failure or that you've forgotten your place, but hold firm. Go at the pace you want, whatever pace you think will engage the audience. But be careful. Too fast and it's a confusion; too slow and they're asleep.

Look the Part

Looking the part is important. It is the claim of this book that in time George W. Bush will be seen as a president who gave exceptionally good and sometimes great speeches. His body language was nearly always mature, strong, and bold and showed leadership with an ability to cope. Yes, he made mistakes. So do all presidents and leaders and that's not really the point here. His stance is very much one of someone in charge. President Richard M. Nixon's body language was always, by comparison, defensive, slightly hunched, and anxious. Obviously this was more particularly so around the time of Watergate and twenty-twenty hindsight is a wonderful thing. But way before that, his stance was suspect.

Consider your body—its shape, how you move, what looks good as a movement, what not. Also consider how much energy you put into movement and gestures. Keep everything simple and, remember, purposeful. Also consider the space you have available. Don't, for instance, stay in one corner or hide perpetually at the back or behind the lectern. Consider the shape of your speech and adjust what you do on stage accordingly. The overall impression one has of a speaker is made up of a mix of the whole look. Confidence, knowledge, and understanding are three core ingredients for which an audience will look and listen. A fourth is how the speaker behaves and manages his or her movement.

One thing that all great speakers do is maintain sincere eye contact with their audiences. Look straight into the eyes of a person in the audience for a few seconds at a time. But don't for goodness' sake stare at the same one throughout your speech, otherwise he or she will think that you have designs on him or her or that there's something terribly wrong. Have direct eye contact with a number of people in the audience, and every now and then glance around at the whole audience while speaking. Use your eye contact to make everyone in your audience feel involved.

Remember too that at a big conference, your face may well be up on large screens at the side or middle of the stage area. Every twitch, smile, scowl, or bead of sweat will be magnified for all to see in great detail. Every scratched chin and wringing of hands will be available for close scrutiny. And now with high definition, every pore of your skin can be observed. You can't do a lot about that, but you can manage your expression and stage behavior.

The Art of Communication

Every communication comprises of two conversations: the verbal content and the body language that accompanies it. When the two are aligned, a speaker can be powerful—even charismatic. When they are not aligned, the audience believes the nonverbal every time. President Obama has the posture of a leader. He strides out to lecterns with the confident and upright bearing of someone in command. But there's more. His wave to an audience has always been that of a leader acknowledging the many. As he begins to speak, Obama nods repeatedly, acknowledging people in the crowd, and building empathy with them. He signals confidence because he's at once alert and yet sufficiently relaxed to show that his nerves (and he'll have some—every speaker does) haven't got the better of him. There is, by the way, an annoying habit delivered by some senior politicians and indeed business executives. As he or she walks to the stage to applause, tumultuous or otherwise, he or she points to imaginary friends in the audience; then he or she points to a particular imaginary friend and offers a big grin. Sometimes this may be a truth; however, mostly one suspects it isn't.

Obama is a polished, powerful, and persuasive speaker. His manner, confident voice, and pace result in accomplished deliveries. When he stood up to make his inaugural speech, the appetite of the immediate audience and the world beyond was not simply to see the 44th president of the United States take office (and all the historic significance attached to that), but to hear him speak. Because he now had a reputation as an orator. People were curious and fascinated. They turned up or tuned in to listen to the methodology of his speech as much as the content. They watched to see a man's bearing and poise as much as they listened to hear his words. That's extraordinary. Ted Sorensen, former speechwriter par excellence to John F. Kennedy, said that words "are the instruments that a president of the United States uses to govern the country and win the support of the world." Beautifully put and absolutely true.

At a mere 278 words, Abraham Lincoln's Gettysburg address, delivered on November 19, 1863, shows that perhaps one of the tricks to the art of great oratory is to be reasonably brief. When Lincoln rose to speak, he faced many thousands of people gathered around Cemetery Hill, the site of heavy Confederate bombardment during the battle. How the multitude thought they'd ever hear much is extraordinary. William Rathvon, then a young boy, later a successful businessman, was a witness to the Lincoln speech. Rathvon left a recording in 1938 which describes the speech and the content. He describes how Lincoln stepped forward and "with a manner serious almost to sadness, gave his brief address." He also made mention of Lincoln's words "echoing through the hills." While the Gettysburg speech was remarkable, Lincoln's voice was often regarded by some as thin and reedy. Noah Brooks writes in *Washington in Lincoln's Time* (1894) that "the [second] inaugural address was received in most profound silence. Every word was clear and audible as the ringing and somewhat shrill tones of Lincoln's voice sounded over the vast concourse." Lincoln knew that oratory was performance as much as persuasion and compensated richly in his speechwriting and body language for a voice that was not always deep or attractive.

The art of oratory is as much about performing as it is about persuading others of the merits of your argument. Thomas Babington Macaulay in his *Essay on Athenian Orators* (1824) said, "The object of oratory alone is not truth, but persuasion." And persuasion comes about by how you perform just as much as by what you say. Pliny the Younger (Caius Caecillius Secundus) wrote in *Epistles* II, 3 (circa 103 B.C.): "Besides, as is usually the case, we are much more affected by the words which we hear, for though what you read in books may be more pointed, yet there is something in the voice, the look, the carriage, and even the gesture of the speaker, that makes a deeper impression upon the mind." Words help us to believe we can achieve great things—either in a small environment (like Ms Shoesmith's) or a large one (like the whole world). Add to the value of words the dynamism of stance and speaker behavior on stage and the result can be powerful and moving.

Cultural Differences

Formality and informality very much relate to how you interact with people from your position as a speaker. If you are presenting to a small group of people who speak and understand English but don't come from an English-speaking country, it's a good idea to establish how people greet each other, how close they stand to one another when talking, and whether they maintain eye contact while talking. In some cultures, such as in German-speaking ones, it's usual to shake hands when meeting and leaving others, even in informal situations. In Latin America, southern-Europe and Arabic-speaking cultures, people often stand much closer together when talking then in English-speaking cultures. Not doing so is seen as unfriendly and odd. Gestures and body language differ from culture to culture. For example, the thumbs-up sign is offensive in Iraq and other Arabic-speaking countries. In France, the ok symbol with thumb and forefinger means "nothing," "rubbish," or "worthless." It can be offensive and downright vulgar in Brazil, Russia and sometimes in Germany. Shaking your head in Bulgaria and Turkey often means "yes" and if you nod your head people in those countries would think that you meant "no." Just to add to your confusion if you nod your head upwards to people from Bulgaria or Turkey they may think that you meant "I don't know."

Amongst many Chinese people it is considered offensive and dismissive to give people things using only one hand—both hands must be used (and by the way that includes giving someone a business card). If you are sitting down on a stage during a Q&A, showing the sole of your foot to, or pointing your foot at, people from the Middle East and South East Asia, is insulting. Amongst Japanese and Korean people blowing your nose in public is considered pretty disgusting and certainly bad manners. In Korea and Arabic-speaking countries, respect for the elderly is very important. They should be greeted first, and be served first in social gatherings. You should also stand up as they enter a room and when speaking to them. These matters are unlikely to be a problem for most speakers but do be careful. A small slip can cause great offence. If in doubt, check.

POINTS TO REMEMBER

- Your body language can influence what audience members think of you.
- Body language, voice and speech content all contribute to your delivery.
- Feel and look relaxed—easier said than done, but important. Try to eradicate any strange movements, nervous hand flutters, face and body scratching and so on. Try to ensure that audience members can see that you're relaxed.
- Don't clutch the lectern for dear life and don't wander the stage or presentation space aimlessly. If you move make the move purposeful.
- Posture is important. Don't slouch or slump. We often (invariably) forget what our body's doing when we're in full flush of public speaking or answering a question. Practice in front of a mirror or ask a close friend for an opinion.
- A pause can be a powerful tool. A pause can be dramatic and can also allow listeners to reflect on what you've just said.
- Make (sincere) eye contact with people in your audience. Smile as appropriate to your topic.
- Oratory is as much about performance as it is about persuading people that your proposition is a right one. Performance without content won't work and words without performance don't either.

Chapter Thirteen
Quote Unquote

"He wrapped himself in quotations—as a beggar would enfold himself in the purple of Emperors."
Rudyard Kipling (1865–1936)

Quotations are often never used by many speakers or overused by an equal number. They can be a powerful speaking tool if used well and with care. Orson Welles, often the cynic, said, "Now we sit through Shakespeare in order to recognize the quotations." Not strictly true perhaps and a little unfair on Shakespeare. Maybe he was unfair on audiences too. But there is truth in the notion that, because quotations of the good and the great (and the bad and the silly) are so readily available on a wide variety of Web sites, they are too often crammed in whenever a speaker might have a gap or where the plot has gone a little awry. They get used as a filler or an amuse bouche. If used as the former, the listeners can lose their way and may not understand where an argument is going or has gone. If used as the latter, then the quotation has to be fun or absolutely relevant to the audience, the event, your topic, something concrete, or again the good listeners won't know what's going on. The downside of this, apart from anything else, is that the audience may feel incompetent or stupid and they won't care for you much for causing that. Ralph Waldo Emerson, that great man of letters and excellent American orator, wrote in his *Journals and Miscellaneous Notebooks* (1849), "I hate quotations. Tell me what you know." It's sometimes clear as to what he meant. Audiences want you and your insights and if all they get are a list of others' opinions, no matter how funny or witty, they might not find you to their liking. Some might say that quotations are a substitute for your own wit. On the other hand, Michel de Montaigne (a French essayist of the Renaissance who influenced many writers who followed) wrote in his *Essais, Book 1* (1580): "I quote others only in order the better to express myself." There's some truth in what Montaigne said. Quoting sensibly and appositely can give your speech interest and depth.

If you accept that "care" is the byword in using quotations, then using them is on the whole beneficial. Using quotations with caution in a speech is indeed an excellent way to improve your credibility and capture the attention and trust of your audience. You can quote a specific something from spoken discourse or literature or indeed another's speech, or you can quote a famous line that suits your cause or argument, perhaps amending it slightly (but declaring that you have) to suit your argument even more. This is a very important point: the quotations you choose should be relevant to your topic and support your argument. Liberal sprinklings of quotations that add nothing—or worse, distract—will diminish your speech. So be careful.

Finding and Using Quotes

Presuming you want to quote other people, where do you find suitable quotes that you can use for speaking assignments? If you do an online search, you'll find millions of resources with vast lists of quotations. Because relevance is key, you should make your search as precise as possible. For example, if you're going to be talking to Sally Shoesmith's colleagues about newly implemented sales targets, you might do a search for quotes, then salesmen and saleswomen, then winners. You could also look for someone who is generally regarded as brilliant or admired in the field in which you have an interest. See what quotes they've contributed, or perhaps quote a line from something that they've written. But it's important that you understand the quote and that it's really right for the context. Don't assume that your audience doesn't know the work of the person you're quoting. Perhaps your audience will know it even better than you.

The pain of misquoting through design or carelessness can be severe. In June 2009, former House speaker Newt Gingrich wrote a new column in a magazine called *Human Events* in which he misquoted a sentence from the American Declaration of Independence. Gingrich, a staunch Reagan supporter, outlined his principles for a Republican return. In the piece, he referred to the Declaration of Independence to support his conservative values. He wrote, "If you go to the National Archives, you will find the words that are fundamental to America written in the Declaration of Independence: 'We are endowed by our creator with certain inalienable rights among which are life, liberty, and the pursuit of happiness.'" The declaration actually reads: "We hold these truths to be self-evident, that all men are created equal, that they are endowed by their Creator with certain unalienable Rights, that among these are Life, Liberty and the pursuit of Happiness." The outcry post-publication was big; the good that Gingrich hoped that his article would do for his cause was dampened and squashed flat.

Another hole in the road is when a speaker uses quotes that are assumed to emanate from a specific source. For example, "If they have no bread, let them eat cake!" (*"S'ils n'ont plus de pain, qu'ils mangent de la brioche."*) is a quote that is frequently attributed to Marie Antoinette. However, she didn't say this. It's actually a quote from Jean-Jacques Rousseau's autobiography, *Confessions* (1782), published after his death in which he wrote: "At length I recollected the thoughtless saying of a great princess, who, on being informed that the country people had no bread, replied, 'Then let them eat brioche!'"

Provide a Context

Quotations won't make your proposition for you; they can only support it. You have to set any quotation in a context. In isolation the quotation will mean very little. The context should set the basic scene for when, possibly where, and under what circumstances the quotation was spoken or written. So, in providing a context, you might write something like: "Gerald Ford was seldom accused of political deftness. But upon taking the oath of office after President Richard Nixon's resignation, he captured the national mood by saying: 'Our long national nightmare is over.'"

Also, tell your audience who is speaking. Don't assume that the listener will know the context or the person who's talking. If it's very obvious then fine, but it's better to spell it out rather than assume. So, you might say something like: "It's hard to remember when President George W. Bush commanded support from the majority of the American people. But on the night of September 11, 2001, he gave a speech that even the hardest Democrats found moving. Commenting on the fact that presidents normally come before a joint session of Congress only for a State of the Union address, Bush began: 'My fellow citizens, for the last nine days, the entire world has seen for itself the state of our union—and it is strong.'"

Read Widely

Don't assume that your listeners will necessarily understand why the quotation you've just used holds significance. Use quotations at strategically selected moments and, if necessary, say why they work for your case. Reading a lot is always going to help in your search for raw material for speeches. Not just management or political books but magazines, newspapers, poetry, short stories, and novels. Serious stuff as well as light material—it all adds to the wealth of what you can use. Be aware of what people are reading at large. Check out what's popular and by whom it's been written. Find out which are the books of the moment; read a few—even if they're not your cup of tea. And find a simple way to keep track of quotation gems, for example, by keeping a notebook of material to use in speeches. If you're not writing your speeches, be sure that whoever is understands your taste and chooses quotes that are appropriate for your personality, subject, and argument. Carrying a notebook sounds slightly old-fashioned, but it is a useful method. If you're in a meeting or even just listening to the radio or watching TV, there's likely to be something that you might want to note down—a witticism or a comment that relates to the day's politics, a funny scenario, an extraordinary fact, a cute word—whatever. Make sure that you take down the quote exactly. Again, bear in mind that there may be people in your audience who know the quote or the fact better than do you.

There was an incident at an international event, a recognized and well-known Swiss congress of the best financial brains in the world. At one breakout session a speaker quoted an expert, and the quote supported his argument superbly well. The quote went something like this, "There will be a reckoning in 2009 and beyond where meltdown will cause the world's economic systems to collapse." A hand shot up in the audience (this was an informal breakout session). "Yes, sir?" said the speaker. The gentlemen to whom the raised hand belonged stood up. "Did you say that xyz said 'there will be a reckoning'?" "Absolutely. Yes," said the speaker with great authority. "You're certain of that?" came the reply (a tad smugly maybe). "Oh, yes." "Well, that's funny," said the questioner, "I was sure that I said 'may' and if you look at the sentences that followed that line in my book called abc published by xyz and available on Amazon at $15.85, you'd see why." Well, of course, everyone laughed or smiled good-naturedly (and perhaps a bit awkwardly), but the damage was well and truly done.

Good Ways of Adding Value to Your Proposition

On your path to becoming a great speaker, you can improve your credibility by aligning yourself with successful, knowledgeable, and respected people in your field. E-mail them, share your views, read their books, tweet them, look up what they're writing about at the moment, and find out who opposes their views and why. Get on the inner circle of ideas.

Also, using humorous quotes can also add entertainment value and put smiles on the faces of your audience. This helps to relax you, the speaker, and makes those to whom you are speaking feel more comfortable. Quoting a funny story, either yours or somebody else's, can be a successful way of opening a speech. But, it does depend on circumstance, and, as you're aware, you need to think carefully about how any humor will be received. There are many, many traps into which you can fall when telling jokes. The rule is simple. Research your audience. Know what makes the people in it tick and create humor that suits that audience. You'll never please everyone all of the time (and you shouldn't try), but obviously your best gags will be the ones that relate to what your audience understands or thinks comedic and appropriate. You really do not want to cause embarrassment, as well as tumbleweed.

Sometimes you may wish to quote statistics. It's a good way to begin a speech. Remember that you can shock your audience; it's often a good opening gambit depending of course on what sort of shock you have in mind. Surprise people. This does not mean that you should put a myriad of stats on a PowerPoint visual. Just tell your audience the powerful and shocking statistic and keep it straightforward. Obviously, relevancy once again is important. Quoting a fact to open a speech is a good way to sum up your theme by getting the immediate attention of your audience. Also, note that you are choosing facts to support your proposition—definitely not to bulk it up. And you should find quotes that are reasonably short, interesting, or simply supportive. Don't automatically look for the Google button either. If you can't find anything that fits, go back to basics and draw on your own personal experiences. This is often the best approach of all.

A Quote Can Work Hard For You

Sometimes a quote can crystallize your proposition, but don't begin with a quote you want to use and then write a speech around it. Many executives do this because they think it's an easy solution and a route to looking good. You know that the whole point of a speech or presentation is to sway your audience or get a certain point across to the people in it. Make that the overriding goal of your speech. Another mistake often made is that quotations are chosen because they look good on paper, even though they don't sound particularly powerful when they're read aloud. Also steer clear of clichéd or crass quotations. If your audience has heard a quote a hundred times before, they're less likely to perk up when they hear it again. This is a general (and obvious) rule. If a famous, well-used quote is simply the most appropriate you can find, make the decision to use it in your presentation certainly, but make it fit in seamlessly. You want to create the impression that your speech is natural and comfortable. Remember, you're an actor. And statements that are crass or in poor taste will undoubtedly be perceived as offensive by at least some members of your audience, and they will likely be turned off, which is something you certainly want to avoid.

Most speechwriters and frequent observers of speechmakers will tell you that many people in any audience will forget around 8 per cent of a speech's content the following day. But amazingly, people in the same audience can repeat a well-chosen quotation or humorous item from a speech—sometimes as long as several years later. If a quotation reinforces the point you want to make, it is almost impossible to misuse it. However, you must make the quotations blend into your natural pattern of delivery. If, for example, you want to quote Cicero but aren't sure if the audience is familiar with Cicero, you can say, "A brilliant Roman orator and politician once said..." John Gardner, secretary of Health, Education, and Welfare under President Johnson, was one of America's most gifted speakers and writers. On November 10, 1990, he gave a speech to a group of management consultants from management consultancy, McKinsey, in Phoenix, Arizona, on the subject of personal renewal, and he used over twenty separate quotations. All of them were blended into what he said as a whole so cleverly that they seemed perfectly natural, each supporting his proposition and argument. Do read it. While it's not as a rule a good idea to use twenty quotations in rapid succession, it worked for him. It's a great example of a great speech. Here's a slice:

"I'm going to talk about some basic problems of the life cycle that will surely hit you if you're not ready for them...Not long ago, I read a splendid article on barnacles...Sometimes days go by without my reading about barnacles, much less remembering what I read. But this article had an unforgettable opening paragraph. 'The barnacle,' the author explained, 'is confronted with an existential decision about where it's going to live. Once it decides, it spends the rest of its life with its head cemented to a rock.'...We've all seen men and women, even ones in fortunate circumstances with responsible positions who seem to run out of steam in midcareer...We have to face the fact that most men and women out there in the world of work are more stale than they know, more bored than they would care to admit...Logan Pearsall Smith said that boredom can rise to the level of a mystical experience and if that's true I know some very busy middle level executives who are among the great mystics of all time."

Quotations are a favorite device of orators. They can make what you say sound good. Sometimes great. Talking of great, Shakespeare is an excellent source for quotations and also has some brilliant examples of oratory from which you can sample material and also learn much about the construction of persuasive speeches. The persuasive form of oratory of course means that the orator is deliberately attempting to sway the audience to his or her perspective. In *Hamlet*, for example, the prince's speech to the players is an oration that is epideictic (one used to praise or blame someone or something). It's also persuasive because it is leading those in the audience through the evidence of blame to move them to Hamlet's side, much as a lawyer might do. *The Merchant of Venice* provides some excellent oratory because sections of it are set in a courtroom, and the entire play is about supporting the prosecution and the defense and then apportioning blame. "The quality of mercy is not strain'd," (act 4, scene 1) from Portia's speech, is a classic and great line, to be used in a variety of circumstances and in a wide variety of contexts. The line is frequently misinterpreted. It means mercy can come easily to those who are naturally merciful, or that mercy can spread far without becoming thin; perhaps "strain'd" means "restraint" or "holding back." Another good line to use (appropriately) is, "This above all: to thine own self be true" (*Hamlet*, act 1, scene 3). It means that one shouldn't deceive oneself. To deceive yourself (kid yourself, lie to yourself, hide behind something else, delude yourself) is sometimes easier than deceiving other people. Anyway, it's not the purpose here to be a reference for all kinds of quotations you could use in a great speech, but Shakespeare is undoubtedly a good resource, and the following can work fabulously well. Have a look at these happy few:

Useful Quotations from the works of Shakespeare

- "The common curse of mankind—folly and ignorance." *Troilus and Cressida*, act 2, scene 3

- "There is nothing either good or bad, but thinking makes it so." *Hamlet*, act 2, scene 2

- "Brevity is the soul of wit." *Hamlet*, act 2, scene 2

- "Do you think I am easier to be played on than a pipe?" *Hamlet*, act 3, scene 2

- "I will speak daggers to her, but use none." *Hamlet*, act 3, scene 2

- "When sorrows come, they come not single spies, but in battalions." *Hamlet*, act 4, scene 5

- "The devil hath power / To assume a pleasing shape." *Hamlet*, act 2, scene 2

- "All the world's a stage, / And all the men and women merely players; / They have their exits and their entrances; / And one man in his time plays many parts." *As You Like It*, act 2, scene 7

- "Can one desire too much of a good thing?" *As You Like It* act 4, scene 1

- "I like this place and willingly could waste my time in it." *As You Like It*, act 2, scene 4

- "Now is the winter of our discontent." *King Richard III*, act 1, scene 1

- "What's in a name? That which we call a rose by any other name would smell as sweet." *Romeo and Juliet*, act 2, scene 2

- "Wisely and slow; they stumble that run fast." *Romeo and Juliet*, act 2, scene 3

- "The better part of valor is discretion." *King Henry IV, Part I,* act 5, scene 4

- "Uneasy lies the head that wears a crown." *King Henry IV, Part II,* act 3, scene 1

- "Defend your reputation, or bid farewell to your good life for ever." *Merry Wives of Windsor,* act 3, scene 2

- "Not that I loved Caesar less, but that I loved Rome more." *Julius Caesar,* act 3, scene 2

- "Friends, Romans, countrymen, lend me your ears; I come to bury Caesar, not to praise him." *Julius Caesar,* act 3, scene 2

- "Cry 'Havoc' and let slip the dogs of war." *Julius Caesar,* act 3, scene 1

- "If any, speak; for him have I offended. I pause for a reply." *Julius Caesar,* act 3, scene 2

And of course there are many, many others—superb lines from a superb writer offering great somethings for most arguments and most occasions. But, granted, Shakespeare isn't for everyone or everything. In looking at any sources for quotations, please do remember to be wary of anything that's a cliché. Here are some other favorite quotes from a wide variety of writers, thinkers, scientists, teachers, philosophers, and politicians:

Other Useful Quotations

- "Glory is fleeting, but obscurity is forever."
  Napoleon Bonaparte (1769–1821)

- "Victory goes to the player who makes the next-to-last mistake."
  Chessmaster Savielly Grigorievitch Tartakower (1887–1956)

- "Don't be so humble—you're not that great."
  Golda Meir (1898–1978), to a visiting diplomat

- "When one person suffers from a delusion it is called insanity; when many people suffer from a delusion it is called religion."
  Robert Pirsig (1948–)

- "Give me chastity and continence, but not yet."
  Saint Augustine (354–430)

- "Not everything that can be counted counts, and not everything that counts can be counted."
  Albert Einstein (1879–1955)

- "Only two things are infinite, the universe and human stupidity, and I'm not sure about the former."
  Albert Einstein

- "A lie gets halfway around the world before the truth has a chance to get its pants on."
  Sir Winston Churchill (1874–1965)

- "I do not feel obliged to believe that the same God who has endowed us with sense, reason, and intellect has intended us to forgo their use."
Galileo Galilei (1564–1642)

- "I'm living so far beyond my income that we may almost be said to be living apart."
e e cummings (1894–1962)

- "Give me a museum and I'll fill it."
Pablo Picasso (1881–1973)

- "Assassins!"
Arturo Toscanini (1867–1957), to his orchestra

- "Each problem that I solved became a rule which served afterwards to solve other problems."
René Descartes (1596–1650)

- "In the end, we will remember not the words of our enemies, but the silence of our friends."
Martin Luther King Jr. (1929–1968)

- "Nothing in the world is more dangerous than sincere ignorance and conscientious stupidity."
Martin Luther King Jr.

- "Try to learn something about everything and everything about something."
Thomas Henry Huxley (1825–1895)

- "The only difference between me and a madman is that I'm not mad."
  Salvador Dali (1904–1989)

- "But at my back I always hear / Time's winged chariot hurrying near."
  Andrew Marvell (1621–1678)

- "Good people do not need laws to tell them to act responsibly, while bad people will find a way around the laws."
  Plato (427–347 B.C.)

- "The power of accurate observation is frequently called cynicism by those who don't have it."
  George Bernard Shaw (1856–1950)

- "Against stupidity, the gods themselves contend in vain."
  Friedrich von Schiller (1759–1805)

- "Never interrupt your enemy when he is making a mistake."
  Napoleon Bonaparte (1769–1821)

- "I think 'Hail to the Chief' has a nice ring to it."
  John F. Kennedy (1917–1963), when asked the name of his favorite song

- "The difference between 'involvement' and 'commitment' is like an eggs-and-ham breakfast: the chicken was 'involved'—the pig was 'committed.'"
  Unknown, but I wish I'd written it

- "If you are going through hell, keep going."
  Sir Winston Churchill

- "God is a comedian playing to an audience too afraid to laugh."
  Voltaire (1694–1778)

- "I have not failed. I've just found 10,000 ways that won't work."
  Thomas Alva Edison (1847–1931)

- "Maybe this world is another planet's Hell."
  Aldous Huxley (1894–1963)

- "Blessed is the man, who having nothing to say, abstains from giving wordy evidence of the fact."
  George Eliot (1819–1880)

- "I've had a wonderful time, but this wasn't it."
  Groucho Marx (1895–1977)

- "It's kind of fun to do the impossible."
  Walt Disney (1901–1966)

- "An inconvenience is only an adventure wrongly considered; an adventure is an inconvenience rightly considered."
  Gilbert Keith Chesterton (1874–1936)

- "The true measure of a man is how he treats someone who can do him absolutely no good."
  Samuel Johnson (1709–1784)

- "All truth passes through three stages. First, it is ridiculed. Second, it is violently opposed. Third, it is accepted as being self-evident."
Arthur Schopenhauer (1788–1860)

- "Many a man's reputation would not know his character if they met on the street."
Elbert Hubbard (1856–1915)

- "If you want to make an apple pie from scratch, you must first create the universe."
Carl Sagan (1934–1996)

- "Once is happenstance. Twice is coincidence. Three times is enemy action."
Auric Goldfinger, in *Goldfinger*, by Ian L. Fleming (1908–1964)

- "To love oneself is the beginning of a lifelong romance."
Oscar Wilde (1854–1900)

- "The nice thing about being a celebrity is that if you bore people they think it's their fault."
Henry Kissinger (1923–)

- "Obstacles are those frightful things you see when you take your eyes off your goal."
Henry Ford (1863–1947)

- Some bumper stickers that appeal:
"Where are we going, and why am I in this handbasket?"
"Ever stop to think, and forget to start again?"

"Three kinds of people: those who can count and those who
can't."

"A bartender is just a pharmacist with a limited inventory."

"A day without sunshine is like, night."

"Don't rub the lamp unless you're ready for the genie."

"Dyslexics of the world, untie."

"If at first you do succeed, try not to look astonished."

- "First they ignore you, then they laugh at you, then they
  fight you, then you win."
  Mahatma Gandhi (1869–1948)

- "The secret of success is to know something nobody else
  knows."
  Aristotle Onassis (1906–1975)

- "I would have made a good Pope."
  Richard M. Nixon (1913–1994)

- "If you haven't got anything nice to say about anybody,
  come sit next to me."
  Alice Roosevelt Longworth (1884–1980)

- "Forgive your enemies, but never forget their names."
  John F. Kennedy

- "Thank you for sending me a copy of your book—I'll waste
  no time reading it."
  Moses Hadas (1900–1966)

- "He who hesitates is a damned fool."
  Mae West (1892–1980)

- "You can pretend to be serious; you can't pretend to be witty."
  Sacha Guitry (1885–1957)

- "Hell is a half-filled auditorium."
  Robert Frost (1874–1963)

- "If I were two-faced, would I be wearing this one?"
  Abraham Lincoln (1809–1865)

- "Now I am become death, the destroyer of worlds."
  Robert J. Oppenheimer (1904–1967), quoting from the *Bhagavad Gita*, after witnessing the first nuclear explosion

- "Attention to health is life's greatest hindrance."
  Plato (427–347 B.C.)

- "Men are not disturbed by things, but the view they take of things."
  Epictetus (A.D. 55–135)

- "Not only is there no God, but try finding a plumber on Sunday."
  Woody Allen (1935–)

- "Never mistake motion for action."
  Ernest Hemingway (1899–1961)

- "Well done is better than well said."
  Benjamin Franklin (1706–1790)

- "Sometimes it is not enough to do our best; we must do what is required."
  Sir Winston Churchill

- "A pessimist sees the difficulty in every opportunity; an optimist sees the opportunity in every difficulty."
  Sir Winston Churchill

- "I think there is a world market for maybe five computers."
  Thomas Watson (1874–1956), chairman of IBM, in 1943

- "Who the hell wants to hear actors talk?"
  H. M. Warner (1881–1958), founder of Warner Brothers, in 1927

- "We don't like their sound, and guitar music is on the way out."
  Decca Recording Co., rejecting the Beatles, in 1962

- "He can compress the most words into the smallest idea of any man I know."
  Abraham Lincoln

- "It is better to be feared than loved, if you cannot be both."
  Niccolo Machiavelli (1469–1527), *The Prince*

- "This isn't right, this isn't even wrong."
  Wolfgang Pauli (1900–1958), upon reading a young physicist's paper

- "If you were plowing a field, which would you rather use? Two strong oxen or 1024 chickens?"
  Seymour Cray (1925–1996), father of supercomputing

And there are a myriad of others for every possible occasion or subject, to help you persuade your audience of your proposition. To help you to speak like a president.

POINTS TO REMEMBER

- Sensibly used, quotations add enormous value to a speech and they will reinforce argument. Or they can add wit and humor and still reinforce an argument.
- There are obviously a huge variety of quotations from which you can choose. Research thoroughly and keep a note of quotations you like even if you don't use them immediately. Remember to keep a note of who said what, why and where.
- Ensure that you understand any quote that you use.
- Always provide a context for the quotation. Quotations can only ever support your proposition; they can't make it.
- It's worth mentioning again—read widely.
- Amusing quotations from or about a famous person are worth collecting as are quotations that relate specifically to your business, politics or hobbies.
- Shakespeare and other great writers are a great source for quotations but don't baffle your audiences.

Chapter Fourteen
Presidential Speechwriters

"The trick of speechwriting, if you will, is making the client say your brilliant words while somehow managing to make it sound as though they issued straight from their own soul."
Christopher Buckley, speechwriter for George H. W. Bush (1952–)

Jon Favreau, Obama's key 2008 campaign speechwriter, is relatively young (born in 1966), but he perfected his understanding of his master's voice as well as Obama's mannerisms in delivery and movement. Because he clearly understands his boss so well, Favreau can clearly imagine precisely how a line would be delivered, how its intonation would work, where the inflection was, and where the voice would be raised or lowered. Having your own writer for your own speeches is a great privilege and many senior business executives and politicians enjoy just such a privilege—although the writers are often managed and utilized poorly. Sometimes the writers are good, sometimes just so-so. Sometimes they are judged to be ready for an exit and are put into the executive writer pool; sometimes, the writers really understand their client; sometimes they couldn't give two hoots. Sometimes the writers will really understand their chiefs' messages, sometimes absolutely not.

The trick of speechwriting, if you are a speechwriter, is making your speechmaker say your extraordinarily fabulous words while somehow managing to make them sound as if they came straight from your speechmaker's own head and heart. For instance, many business people and American (mostly Democratic) politicians have tried to evoke the Kennedy brothers, but the writing of any speech has to suit the speaker and, to become great, has to appear both natural and brilliant in messaging and chemistry. Obama had more success than most. It helped and helps of course that Obama has the Kennedy élan as well as a photogenic family. One supposes that we can't dismiss the latter element in politics and, increasingly, in business, although too much can put off listeners and viewers. And it's an unfortunate truth that many a brilliant politician has lost a cause or an election because of a receding hairline, other facial issue, or look. Stupid but, unfortunately in this media world, so.

Great speechwriters understand, of course, the core elements of great speech creation. They know, for instance, that any audience—small or large, bright or dim—will have too much information overload on a daily basis. Speech content therefore must be simple and slightly underdone or even rare—certainly not overcooked. Many in any audience will be thinking about different issues, so the speaker must be brilliant—to entertain, to focus, to attract, to focus again, to inform, to direct, to persuade. All in the audience will be able to think faster than anyone can speak. We all think at roughly 600 words a minute, and on average people talk at 140 words per minute. So, if the audience understands a point really quickly, then the scriptwriter needs to make the manner by which an audience hears the point and its affirmation interesting and very easy on the ear.

To Write a Great Speech, Writers Need to Understand Listening

Active listening is very hard work, exhausting in fact. When you're actively listening, your respiration rate goes up and your heart starts to beat faster. People can't (and won't) do that for long, so to keep them in the room, so to speak, they need a mental and aural break such as visual material, humor, change of pace, or audience interaction. However serious a topic, any audience wants to be entertained. There are just degrees, that's all. Sometimes audiences, or large quantities of people within audiences, just don't listen. They disengage for a whole host of reasons. Fifty percent of people in the world have hearing problems to a greater or lesser degree. Regional language differences, poorly taught language, simultaneous translations, and accents can all create barriers or confusion. Audiences sometimes assume that speakers, even great ones, said or implied something they didn't. And audiences don't always recognize the benefits of a proposition that you or your scriptwriter think are obvious.

But it's inspiration that can make or break a speech whether or not every word is understood or heard. It's inspiration that a speechwriter can add to your persona and your material. The basics have to be there—you still need to be a great speaker. You still need the single proposition. A speech can evolve out of one line or a phrase, and that's not so abnormal considering the power of a single-minded proposition. That's not the same as relying on one line with no content or argument to back it up. In a December 2008 Washington Post article by Eli Saslow ("Helping to Write History"), Favreau is quoted as saying: "A speech can broaden the circle of people who care about this stuff. How do you say to the average person that's been hurting: 'I hear you, I'm there? Even though you've been so disappointed and cynical about politics in the past, and with good reason, we can move in the right direction. Just give me a chance.'" Favreau wrote an opening line for a post-caucus speech: "They said this day would never come." He later commented: "I knew that it would have multiple meanings to multiple people" and added that "Barack and I talked about it and it was one that worked for the campaign. There were many months during the campaign when they said he'd never win. And of course there was the day that would never come, when an African-American would be winning the first primary in a white state." If you read any of the speeches in which the line appears, it's always surrounded by careful argument and a simple rationale (depending on the audience) as to why the line has meaning and relevance. You can do this too, no matter what the occasion. You must know your proposition and your argument for it and, don't forget, against it. If you know all this, you can choose a line, a phrase, a sound bite to which all your argument can relate—that's a campaign winner, and it's also a great basis upon which to wow Sally Shoesmith.

Presidential Scriptwriters

According to two former presidential speechwriters, Ray Price (Nixon) and Ted Sorensen (Kennedy), most US presidents had speechwriting help. Even George Washington sought some editorial assistance from Alexander Hamilton. But Calvin Coolidge was the first president to hire an official, full-time "professional" speechwriter. Since then, each American president has had an Office of Speechwriting. George W. Bush's speechwriting team was led by (the impressively titled Director of Speechwriting) Michael Gerson (also as it happens a great fan of Jon Favreau and vice versa). At that time there was also a development—the employment of specialist full-time speechwriters who could craft a speech on a particular topic. David Frum, for example, was George W. Bush's economic speech specialist. Many assume now that presidents and leaders in general don't have much to do with their speeches. That may be true. And, indeed, how much does a president contribute to his own speeches? One must suppose that that varies according to the president and a particular speech. Nixon, for example, understood (and was generally good) at debates; he usually felt comfortable without a prepared text, certainly in his early days as president—less so when times became tough. Kennedy, of course, made Ted Sorensen's job easier because of his eloquence and ability to speak in public so very well.

Even if the president *doesn't* write his own text, he will more likely than not influence the speech. That should be the minimum involvement whatever the nature of the speech. Having no involvement is lazy, arrogant, and possibly disastrous; the speeches will gradually become tired, repetitive, and generally poor. There is every good reason why one should ponder the writing of American presidential speeches. The reason is that they are on the whole so very good. Mostly, they would be impossible (well, not impossible perhaps) to deliver badly, and they really are a shining example of what great speechwriting should be. Look at these examples. First is Lincoln's second inaugural address, given on March 4, 1865: "With malice toward none, with charity for all, with firmness in the right as God gives us to see the right, let us strive on to finish the work we are in, to bind up the nation's wounds, to care for him who shall have borne the battle and for his widow and his orphan, to do all which may achieve and cherish a just and lasting peace among ourselves and with all nations." Then, try out in front of a mirror Franklin D. Roosevelt's inaugural address, from March 4, 1933: "So, first of all, let me assert my firm belief that the only thing we have to fear is fear itself—nameless, unreasoning, unjustified terror which paralyzes needed efforts to convert retreat into advance." And the perennial but still fabulous phrasing of John F. Kennedy's inaugural, from January 20, 1961: "And so, my fellow Americans, ask not what your country can do for you—ask what you can do for your country. My fellow citizens of the world, ask not what America will do for you, but what together we can do for the freedom of man." There are many rich examples. American presidents have spoken some of their most memorable words at inaugurations. That's not surprising really—a fresh start always brings out strong speeches in any situation or cause. The same applies in business and most other walks of life.

Not all presidents need a fully fleshed speech. Nixon didn't. Some want the whole thing, word for word. Some speeches are written with a certain formula in mind. For example, some presidential speeches, particularly inaugurals, are almost religious in nature; the seemingly gentle transfer of power they represent is one of the key elements that have made America the oldest surviving democracy. An inaugural speech should both help heal the divisions and schisms of the past campaign (usually highly acrimonious and volatile) and set the direction for the new administration (now presenting a different view from that of the past). An inaugural is also examined closely not only in the United States, but among governments and in households around the world. With America still the world's policeman, the world is, whatever your politics, really among America's constituencies and, to some degree at least, among its responsibilities. So, such a speech needs to be uplifting, yet also realistic. It should never promise what can't be delivered. But it should speak, in those clever words of Abraham Lincoln, to "the better angels of our nature," even as it summons people to those exertions required to achieve the future a president seeks. An inaugural speech should be visionary and for everyone while a State of the Union address should be more domestic and specific in describing legislation.

A big difference in speechwriting during these blog and text days, compared with the more rhetorical days of fifty or sixty years ago, is that attention spans have been radically reduced. With an inauguration or similar speeches of state or occasion, the inherent drama of the ceremony itself gives a little more leeway. The speaker, maybe a president, has to say enough so that people feel he or she has taken the occasion, the opportunity, and them seriously. But a time limit in most instances and on most speaking occasions is a useful discipline; it forces the speaker to focus on the big, central themes and also makes it more likely that the audience will remember those themes. Writing for any speech requires an understanding of that focus. Make sure that your scriptwriters understand your focus and that of your audience. If you're writing your speech, ensure that you do. Remember, when we read great speeches, we just know that the crafted words will have made their mark and created a result.

Not Every Great Speech is the Same

Each president of the United States has used speechwriters differently. They may write first drafts for the president to fine-tune, or provide phrases and slogans, or translate complicated policy proposals into language for a mass audience. We know that Abraham Lincoln wrote the Gettysburg Address and Emancipation Proclamation on his own. Woodrow Wilson, who had written books and professorial articles, also wrote his own speeches. Franklin Roosevelt used several speechwriters, and Dwight Eisenhower began the trend of using journalists, in his case Emmet Hughes. Apart from Sorensen, other Kennedy speechwriters included historian Arthur M. Schlesinger Jr., ambassador to India John Kenneth Galbraith, and White House aide Richard Goodwin. Ronald Reagan relied heavily on Peggy Noonan, one of the first women speechwriters in the White House. Several presidential speechwriters have written important memoirs about the presidencies in which they served and these are worth reading or dipping into to gain insight into speechwriting and the scenarios around the craft. These include Robert Sherwood (*Roosevelt and Hopkins*, 1948), Samuel Rosenman (*The Roosevelt I Knew*, 1946), Emmet Hughes (*Ordeal of Power*, 1962, which is about his years as aide and speechwriter to Eisenhower), Theodore Sorensen (*Kennedy*, 1965), Arthur M. Schlesinger Jr. (*A Thousand Days*, 1965, again, about Kennedy and his court), and William Safire (*Before the Fall: An Inside View of the Pre-Watergate White House*, 1975). There are others, but these, in particular, offer terrific insights and are well written. It's also of more than passing interest to see a little of what goes into great speechwriting from those who wrote some of the greatest speeches.

The Kennedy/Sorenson partnership in speech preparation and writing was a great one; such agreeable speech relationships are rare. Understanding and respect was key. It was always agreed that Kennedy's speeches would contain easy words to speak and understand. Clauses and sentences would also be short and to the point. Clarity was a must, as was use of powerful phrases. Kennedy had no appetite for rosy prose and messy explanations. He liked better a good, crisp, cool, clear argument. It's well known that he liked alliteration and one-liners that reinforced an overall message. It's also what his audiences and the world wanted. Most of Kennedy's sharp, alliterative phrases were created, according to Sorensen, not just for show but to help audiences recall messages. Kennedy's taste for musical and lyrical phrases, like "never negotiating out of fear, but never fearing to negotiate," was evident in most of his speeches, and his audiences loved to listen to them partly for that reason. Kennedy and Sorensen took the process of speechmaking and speechwriting very seriously. Now, not every Wednesday morning sales meeting with Sally Shoesmith requires an inaugural speech—but preparation and lots of practice are crucial in any scenario.

The Writer and the Orator

Jon Favreau is, as Obama himself has put it, the president's mind reader. Again, the team is a good one. For a politician whose rise to prominence was largely built upon his powers as an orator, Obama is well versed in the arts of speechmaking, but a good speechmaker needs a good writer. A fairly recent presidential speech that attracted worldwide attention and had a serious impact on the course of current events was President George W. Bush's Axis of Evil speech, delivered in January 2002 as the State of the Union address. With the Cold War over, the speech called back memories of Ronald Reagan's Evil Empire speech. Apparently, the phrase "axis of hatred" was used initially but "hatred" was later changed to "evil." Once again, politics aside, the short phrase catches the limelight. And, again, there was precedent because Roosevelt had had the same difficulty in 1941 when the United States had been attacked by Japan, while the bigger and tougher threat actually came from Germany. In Bush's speech, Iraq, Iran, and North Korea were tied in to terrorism and wrapped up as one world danger, and they have remained there since. Right or wrong, a speech did that. The thing is, that whatever action you decide upon or whatever proposition you postulate or whatever argument you trade, the explanation needs presenting superbly to your "world." Just as any president has to explain "it" (whatever "it" is) to the American people and the world.

Employing a speechwriter is not vain or lazy but is recognition of the pressures facing business executives, politicians, proud fathers of the bride, the eulogy maker, the deliverer of a fifteen minute presentation to Sally Shoesmith's faithful team. There are times of course when writing your own words is important but even then some support and help from another wordsmith can help to focus and take a litmus test on anecdotes, humor or content. Writing a great speech is hard. Delivering a great speech is hard. Both are areas on which you can seek help and support. Speaking like a president needs a strong sense of self-worth, a strong sense of purpose and a positive outlook. So, go and be great.

POINTS TO REMEMBER

- A speechmaker's task is to make his or her words sound as if they came straight from the speechmaker's head and heart.
- People in any audience think faster than any speaker can speak. Listeners can understand difficult points if presented well.
- A good writer can come up with a memorable line but also (most importantly) the argument to support it. But, if you are writing your own speech, you can do this too. Indeed, you must.
- A writer can't write a great speech without any involvement from the speaker.

- Some speakers will not need a fully fleshed out script. Sometimes, and often invariably, bullet points will suffice. If the bullet points are focused and if you know your topic and argument, then this shouldn't be a problem at all.
- Great speaker/writer partnerships (think Kennedy/ Sorenson or Obama/Favreau) are rare, but when they exist they are an unbeatable recipe for successful and great public speaking. Understanding and respect are vital to this.

Chapter Fifteen
Speak Like a President

"A man whose father less than sixty years ago might not have been served at a local restaurant can now stand before you to take a most sacred oath."
Barack Obama, inauguration speech (1961–)

It's interesting how the difference between speaking like a president and not is a very thin dividing line. All presidents and officers of state and business make mistakes. We've seen some of these earlier. And there's the Reuters-reported gaffe by Hilary Clinton in Brussels (March 6, 2009). Apparently she "raised eyebrows on her first visit to Europe as secretary of state when she mispronounced her EU counterparts' names and claimed US democracy was older than Europe's." Or there's the now famous or infamous George W. Bush line from November 2000, when in Arkansas he said, "They misunderestimated me." And there was the January 2000 comment on education when Bush said, "Rarely is the question asked: is our children learning?" Warren Harding's poor grasp of the English language, along with his insistence on writing his own speeches, produced notorious linguistic gaffes. He is alleged to have once said: "I would like the government to do all it can to mitigate, then, in understanding, in mutuality of interest, in concern for the common good, our tasks will be solved." Bill Clinton's leadership career was, in the view of many, put on severe hold by his address to the 1988 Democratic Convention. Governor Clinton delivered an infamous thirty-minute speech that bored delegates and viewers. When he finally said, "in conclusion" the audience broke out in applause. And we know that there are many other moments where speakers, some great, made mistakes. Speaking like a president is something that can be learned. It will always be the case that any speaker, no matter how great, will from time to time make mistakes, errors of speaking judgment and a number of faux pas. But, if you consider the great speeches that exist in our memories, then those errors, as long as they are occasional, can be excused. Great speakers build a reputation. Whether this is from short speeches on the departure from the office of a colleague or the closing remarks after a day's worth of management conference, you will build a reputation for speaking well if you spend time in creating great delivery and great argument. Once a reputation has been built, you have to keep the momentum going.

A President Speaks

Why is Obama's inauguration speech regarded by some as only so-so? Well, Obama had done so very well with his speeches up to that point in all situations. On TV and on stage people had been wowed by his rhetoric and oratory. Some pundits felt that the inaugural was less than excellent, but then that was by comparison to his recent body of work rather than by the fact that the speech was bad. Some observers regarded it as not as well constructed or as well delivered as his usual fare. On the other hand, as is usually the case with these things, there are a large number of people who believe that Obama succeeded extraordinarily well in his inauguration speech using a simple structure. For example:

- To begin with he thanks his predecessor, and this isn't such a bad place to start—to thank the person who's introduced you or called the meeting or who's facilitating the event—pick someone, even if it's Sally Shoesmith. It behoves you well to show gratitude at the start. In the first two paragraphs of Obama's speech, he thanks George W.

Bush—as a mark of respect for the previous incumbent of the post regardless of his beliefs. Just good manners really.

- Obama is blunt and absolutely to the point about the severe economic crisis. He is honest about its seriousness, using phrases like "the challenges...are real. They are serious and they are many." None of the comments here are promises or even made to measure and ready solutions; they are observations and commitments that these issues need to be managed, and he declares that they will be managed under his guidance and leadership. The comments are not sugarcoated—they display a firm resolve: "But know this, America—they will be met." Strong, simple phraseology is used supported by argument. It's interesting that where there is insufficient argument, the audience will probably realize from previous speeches that it will come soon.

- Obama declares that Americans have often faced tough times, very tough times, and have always overcome them—one way or another. He is consistent with his message of hope that won him the election. He is speaking directly to millions of Americans who feel the "sapping of confidence across our land." He refers to scripture and the Declaration of Independence, then reminds his audience of the struggles of the past that America overcame. He acknowledges that these struggles were tough, but his point is that his job is to ensure that the current issues faced by the US will be met and solved.

- Obama faces up to the cynics and the harsh critics whom he knows existed throughout the campaign and will undoubtedly exist in the future. In an attempt to persuade those who are dubious about his plans, the key phrase here is "Their memories are short." This approach is clever because, by isolating the criticism, he makes it clear that he is aware of it and acknowledges that doubt is normal. It's a good method in a speech to get the majority of an audience on your side by showing that you are openly aware of your critics and that you know what they have to say.

- Obama addresses the wider world about wider world issues. His phrases are powerful yet friendly. With new plans it's a good idea to make them sound warm and natural although you can't sugarcoat hard facts otherwise you'll sound disingenuous. Obama charts a new foreign policy anchored on straightforward, principled, human ideals. It is a paragraph or two on hope, and the message is one that any audience would want to hear, particularly in a nation deeply entrenched in two major wars.

- It's another good device to declare that you can't deliver change all on your own. You need your audience's support and that of their colleagues too. In his inaugural, Obama declares that he will only be able to manage and lead if the American people support his plans, giving him and his administration an opportunity to make good anything which isn't. He mentions, as must you in this situation, that this isn't something that can all happen straight away but you must set a date by which change will begin or will have happened. You also have to spell out what this change will look like. Throughout the inaugural, Obama's connecting devices are terrific, allowing for one topic to merge seamlessly to the next. He also draws parallels between one part of society and another, for example between citizens who are in the armed forces and citizens who are not. His point is that everyone has a duty of service. It is of course reminiscent of John F. Kennedy. This is a call to action, as it was then.

The inaugural doesn't have the sharp edge that many of Obama's speeches have and possibly that's why some didn't see it as a strong case with the fire of oratory that the election speeches had brought. It could be argued that Obama's inaugural address speech was also softer for an audience and a nation that was faced with two wars and a world economic crisis. Without trying to fool the audience or to coat a message with sugar, the speech balanced the reality of the present with hope for the future. There are wonderful and memorable phrases such as "a nation cannot prosper long when it favors only the prosperous." Or the striking challenge to America's enemies: "We will extend a hand if you are willing to unclench your fist." And the now famous: "Starting today, we must pick ourselves up, dust ourselves off, and begin again the work of remaking America."

Strong Propositions Are So Important

You can see that, in Obama's inaugural, shape and straightforward propositions are important. Message is obviously important too, as is clever phraseology. There was no, "Ask not what your country can do for you," "I have a dream," "This was their finest hour," or even "Yes we can." Instead we had a new set of ideas with which Obama wanted America to take home. He wanted his administration and the American people to "begin again the work of remaking America." He wanted Americans to know that what he had to say wasn't just a collection of statements but also an acknowledgement that things needed fixing. He wanted Americans to be aware that he knew about their concerns (and this is important for any speech): "The question we ask today is not whether our government is too big or too small, but whether it works." And the immediate and national audience wanted to hear about leadership, as of course did the wider world, in particular America's friends: "(We) are ready to lead once more."

Barack Obama and Martin Luther King Jr.

A good device used in this inaugural was the amplification of certain words or phrases contrasted with their opposites. This technique—highlighting a concept by remarking on an opposite—was also characteristic of speeches given by Martin Luther King Jr. Obama included phrases with a poetical feel such as: "rising tides of prosperity and the still waters of peace" and "gathering clouds and raging storms." In many ways, this speech, like others of Obama's, is similar to King's "I Have a Dream" speech. Again, the historical context is emphasized in order to target a brighter future. King also offers models for great speechwriting and delivery—not just highly quotable phrases. Anaphora (that is, the repetition of words at the beginning of neighboring clauses) is a rhetorical device often used by King. Repeating the words twice sets the pattern, and further repetitions emphasize that same pattern and increase the rhetorical effect. "I have a dream" is repeated in eight successive sentences and is one of the most often quoted examples of anaphora in any modern speech. There are other occasions where anaphora is evident: "One hundred years later," and "We can never be satisfied," and "With this faith," and the extraordinary "Let freedom ring." You can read these phrases and more or less have the gist of King's speech. With repetition the story becomes clearer and clearer. And, as was the intent, memorable.

Word repetition is typical of a King speech, but it's also a clever method of pushing a point, particularly if used in a challenging way rather than in a manner which irritates or annoys—as is the case with some modern political speeches. Also, don't forget that King was a preacher and repetition was and is usual in most sermons. The most commonly used noun in his speech is "freedom." This makes sense, of course given his topic in most speeches and its use becomes part of the anthem-like quality of the speech. Other words that populate the speech are "nation," "America," "justice," "injustice," and "dream."

King draws on his skills and training as a Baptist minister, quoting primarily from the Bible. He also evokes historic scenes to make a point about now or the future. He uses allusion with regularity and to brilliant effect: "Five score years ago" relates to Lincoln's famous Gettysburg Address, which began "Four score and seven years ago." This allusion is appropriate given that King was speaking in front of the Lincoln Memorial. In your own speeches consider context, time, and place. Biblical allusions provide a moral compass for King's proposition: "It came as a joyous daybreak to end the long night of their captivity" alludes to Psalms 30:5; and "Let us not seek to satisfy our thirst for freedom by drinking from the cup of bitterness and hatred" evokes Jeremiah 2:13. King knew his audiences. He knew that they would understand the biblical allusions, and he knew that the quotations would reinforce a point and tap into his listeners' emotions.

Clever devices or indeed any devices are fine and do have merit. But don't forget that logical, grounded, and specific examples are important to illustrate your points and bring them home to your audience. The preacher King does this, for example, by mentioning American places throughout the speech. Their use familiarizes the listener with the content and makes it real: Mississippi, New York, Alabama, South Carolina, Georgia, Louisiana, New Hampshire, Pennsylvania, Colorado, California, Tennessee. The language of geography is used by King to embrace his audiences completely, in a way that he knows they will understand. It's emotional and it's inclusive and people liked it: "slums and ghettos of our northern cities," "from every mountainside," and "from every village and every hamlet." Metaphors too were part of the King speech toolkit. He used them to join together or contrast concepts that otherwise might just become lost. For example, "joyous daybreak to end the long night of their captivity"; "The Negro lives on a lonely island of poverty in the midst of a vast ocean of material prosperity"; "This sweltering summer of the Negro's legitimate discontent will not pass until there is an invigorating autumn of freedom and equality"; and "sweltering with the heat of oppression, will be transformed into an oasis of freedom and justice." Note the phrases that contrast: "joyous daybreak" and "long night"; "lonely island" and "vast ocean." The pictures he paints are strong and vivid. In your speeches, you don't always have to paint such vivid pictures, but certainly you should be clear, and if the use of contrasting metaphors helps reinforce your argument and creates a vivid scene, use them.

What Presidents Say

In considering how a president might or might not speak, it's useful to have some references up your sleeve. Presidents talk much about liberty and freedom, and such topics can be used to flavor or support many an argument. For example, George Washington said, "Liberty, when it begins to take root, is a plant of rapid growth." He also said, "It will be found an unjust and unwise jealousy to deprive a man of his natural liberty upon the supposition he may abuse it." And, "If the freedom of speech is taken away, then dumb and silent we may be led, like sheep to the slaughter." Thomas Jefferson said about liberty and freedom (and remember that this was the eighteenth century): "I would rather be exposed to the inconveniences attending too much liberty than those attending too small a degree of it." And, "Timid men prefer the calm of despotism to the tempestuous sea of liberty." Here's another great Jefferson line: "The natural progress of things is for liberty to yield and government to gain ground." Then there's Abraham Lincoln, who said, "Freedom is the last, best hope of earth." And, "Those who deny freedom to others deserve it not for themselves." One more, "America will never be destroyed from the outside. If we falter and lose our freedoms, it will be because we destroyed ourselves." Franklin D. Roosevelt said, "We look forward to a world founded upon four essential human freedoms. The first is freedom of speech and expression...The second is freedom of every person to worship God in his own way...The third is freedom from want...The fourth is freedom from fear...anywhere in the world." And another, "We, and all others who believe in freedom as deeply as we do, would rather die on our feet than live on our knees."

You can pick a thread from the speeches of others with which to arm your speeches, or you can refer back to the greats in order to reinforce your argument and support your proposition. And, of course, it's not just American leaders who have led the way with remarks from which you can source supporting comment. In all parts of the world there is a history of oratory.

If you do find it useful to look at American leadership, there's the source of supply that is John F. Kennedy. Be careful here because JFK has long been quoted perhaps overmuch and you need to make your quotes count. There are a few that are less well known: "The unity of freedom has never relied on uniformity of opinion." Or, "The cost of freedom is always high, but Americans have always paid it. And one path we shall never choose, and that is the path of surrender, or submission." And, "In the long history of the world, only a few generations have been granted the role of defending freedom in its hour of maximum danger. I do not shrink from this responsibility—I welcome it." Then there's Ronald Reagan with the powerful and moving, "We will always remember. We will always be proud. We will always be prepared, so we will always be free."

Most presidents have also commented on the strength of democracy. Clinton did, as did both presidents Bush. And there are lines that hit hard right now, for example, "Today we are engaged in a deadly global struggle for those who would intimidate, torture, and murder people for exercising the most basic freedoms. If we are to win this struggle and spread those freedoms, we must keep our own moral compass pointed in a true direction." That's Barack Obama, in firm control of his argument and speaking like a president.

And There's Poetic Language

The greatest speeches often incorporate poetic language, but if you follow suit be careful that the moments or occasions are appropriate.

One example of a poetic and powerful speech is the Tryst with Destiny, delivered to the Constituent Assembly of India in New Delhi on the eve of Indian independence on August 14, 1947. Made by Jawaharlal Nehru, independent India's first prime minister, the speech has a strong beginning and demands immediate attention. It also begins as if he is telling a warm story: "Long years ago we made a tryst with destiny and now the time comes when we shall redeem our pledge, not wholly or in full measure, but very substantially. At the stroke of the midnight hour, when the world sleeps, India will awake to life and freedom. A moment comes, which comes but rarely in history, when we step out from the old to the new, when an age ends, and when the soul of a nation, long suppressed, finds utterance." The speech obviously marks a historic moment and is considered by many in modern India to capture the essence of the country's hundred-year struggle for freedom. The language is very much that of a great tale. The structure is well crafted and, like many stories, contains promise and a clear moral vision. Now, Nehru's words are often copied by business executives and politicians, in setting out their own visions and missions for the futures of their companies or political parties.

The skillful way in which Nehru struck a balance suitable for describing the historic moment and telling a national story is extraordinary. Here is a new day dawning for a new country. Here a people have moved from darkness to light, from oppression (some felt) to freedom. He articulated the remaining struggles and emphasized the fact that these struggles would be more than hard. This is an eloquent and musical speech, one that presents its themes clearly and powerfully. It is rightly regarded as one of the best ever, and even today many Indian children learn it by heart. So it comes as a bit of a surprise to learn that Nehru began his political career as a very hesitant public speaker, and speechmaking was something he had to force himself to learn. Often he would read political speeches and listen to politicians on the radio. By 1947, he had learned to speak smoothly and gently, using colorful and expressive language to suit any occasion.

Despite preparing and rehearsing his speeches, Nehru made himself skilled at making them sound as if they had been made up on the spot. That's a good device and audiences respond well to it—a natural delivery. People also liked his contagious passion and delight: "The appointed day has come—the day appointed by destiny—and India stands forth again, after long slumber and struggle, awake, vital, free and independent." This is vibrant, crisp, and demanding of attention. But it still sounds natural and unforced. Nehru produced several memorable phrases for example, "at the stroke of the midnight hour," "when the world sleeps, India will awake to life and freedom," "a moment comes, which comes but rarely in history," "freedom and power bring responsibility," "the noble mansion of free India where all her children may dwell." But he also supported the passionate proposition (freedom) with argument.

POINTS TO REMEMBER

- Great speakers build a reputation over time. Occasionally, they also make mistakes, get things wrong, mispronounce something, misunderstand someone; too many errors can be damaging.
- Barack Obama's inauguration speech was (perhaps unfairly) not regarded as strong as some of his other campaign speeches. But, it's a great speech by any standard. If you study great speeches, particularly modern ones, you will discover the use of language, oratorical devices, mood, tone, and expression. You can gain good guidance in the use of phraseology and accurate language.

- Great speeches show how an argument can be shaped and what tools are available to shape arguments well.
- Comparisons and similarities between, for example, Barack Obama's speeches and those of Martin Luther King Jr. can help you to focus on how to make a case.
- Many presidents and leaders (of states, nations and businesses) use insights into topics such as freedom and fairness from which we can and should learn.
- Poetic language is powerful but be careful where and when you use it.

Conclusion

"Besides, as is usually the case, we are much more
affected by the words which we hear, for though
what you read in books may be more pointed, yet
there is something in the voice, the look, the carriage
and even the gesture of the speaker, that makes a
deeper impression upon the mind."
Pliny the Younger (A.D. 61–approx A.D. 112) *Epistles* (2.3)

Every nation, state, school, business, college, and social group will
witness good speeches at some time or other. Occasionally, there
will be a great speech. Then, people will hear some brilliant oratory
and the words will cause happiness, reassurance, understanding,
motivation, clarity, or occasionally, hate. Whatever the purpose and
outcome, people in small, large, or huge groups, face-to-face or via
television, will witness focused argument and propositions beautifully
expressed. People will hear, understand and feel something
different.

We can glean good examples of oratory from those in front of the
cameras and on the front pages, even though, invariably in such
situations, any speech and any debate can be inimical to oratory.
Sometimes we will hear something special. In the UK, on May 11
2010, David Cameron became the new British prime minister. Aside
from the politics, his first speech outside 10 Downing Street in
London (the prime minister's formal residence) was superb. Without
notes (although undoubtedly he will have written notes earlier and
will have rehearsed albeit briefly and probably in an official limousine)
Cameron's speech was to the point, beautifully delivered, comfortably
paced and argued with great care and respect to people of all
political persuasions. The phraseology throughout the short speech

was great and the construction of what he said was crisp and apposite for the moment: "Yes, that's [the task of rebuilding trust in the UK's political system] about cleaning up expenses; yes, that's about reforming parliament; and yes, it's about making sure people are in control and that the politicians are always their servants and never their masters." There were shades of Obama and even some of John F. Kennedy in parts of the speech. For instance, Cameron said, "I want to help try and build a more responsible society here in Britain. One where we don't just ask what are my entitlements, but what are my responsibilities?" He added, "One where we don't ask what am I just owed, but more what can I give?" This is clearly reminiscent of Kennedy's "Ask not what your country can do for you." Now, as was the case over fifty years ago, the construction, the message, and delivery are memorable. Cameron followed up with an adept (and guaranteed to be oft quoted) clever line: "And a guide for that society—that those that can should, and those who can't we will always help." Pundits have long agreed that Cameron's speechmaking skills are excellent; indeed it is said that he won the leadership of the Conservative Party in 2005 because of a superb, well-argued, passionate speech he made without notes at the Party conference. He has a gift for language most certainly, but he knew that this occasion wasn't the time for lengthy or fancy rhetoric.

Part of the skill of any great speaker is to get the language, tone, approach and delivery right for a specific occasion. Indeed, it was Hillary Clinton who said in early 2008 (quoting New York Mayor Mario Cuomo) that "you campaign in poetry but you govern in prose." Public speaking isn't easy and delivering great speeches is harder still. But you *can* deliver a great speech if you want to. You need to believe, you need to prepare and you need to practice.

Walk into the studio, dining room, wedding reception, auditorium, conference center, Sally Shoesmith's meeting room, or legislative chamber with your head held high. You have something important to say. *Be* a president. Certainly, it's not always easy. George

Washington never spoke publicly for more than ten minutes because his false teeth required him to keep his jaws clamped tight shut, yet his lofty rhetoric (within, one imagines, ten-minute slots) established the presidency as a dignified institution. John Adams once held Congress spellbound throughout an extraordinary seven-hundred-word sentence (that may have been because of the delivery of such a sentence rather than the oratory, although Adams spoke beautifully and with great charisma). Harry Truman's speeches were dry, halting, and disconnected until he threw away his script and talked off the cuff in a much more natural, down-to-earth, and direct style. For every Washington or Adams, however, there is a Thomas Jefferson—otherwise a president of some brilliance, but who was such a bad public speaker that he refused to deliver a State of the Union address to Congress, instead beginning a century-long tradition of sending congressional members a letter. Then there is George W. Bush, for whom more people will have more time as time goes on. It's true that while many of his speeches were truly excellent, he did have a knack of making up interesting phrases and words. The inventor of new words is a neologist, and Bush was probably one of the best. Good for him, but maybe not so good for a president. But some of his speeches *will* be remembered for their depth and insight. And don't forget, we all make mistakes and so too do orators. Audiences know when an orator is authentic. The orator has to know it too.

One thing Barack Obama does better than many others is to come across as being authentic and thoughtful. He also seems to be present in the moment. He's not just reading a script, and he's not just going through the motions. He gives the impression that he's thinking hard about what he's saying and considering the effect upon the audience. He's engaged and he seems to care. He's trying hard to tell a story, to make communication work, and he's tried hard over time to deliver well-argued propositions. Because he's in politics, it doesn't always work. The best of orators may not always get their way or convince an audience that this direction is better than that or that some idea is more worthwhile than another. The best speakers see the public-speaking opportunity as a two-way street. Sometimes it's one way, and the result is not mutually comfortable. That's the risk of speaking in public.

The Twitter age and the sound-bite methodology of tabloid (and, increasingly, not so tabloid) journalism might have killed oratory. The fact that readers and listeners like the short and the sharp rolling news message might lead one to believe that speechmaking has disappeared. Great speakers and great speeches haven't disappeared. We still need both and we like both. When the electricity doesn't work or the stage is a flatbed truck (as it was for Bobby Kennedy when he gave a short but mesmeric speech announcing the death of Martin Luther King Jr.), then orators come into their own. When times are very hard and when people need leadership and guidance, explanation and clarity—then great speakers in all walks of life come into their own. Oratory, once mighty and strong, has definitely diminished, but it is returning—in politics and in business. Being able to deliver a brilliant speech brilliantly is important because it gives you, whoever you are, a superb opportunity to connect with a target audience on a particular topic about which you care deeply. Whatever you do and whatever you think of yourself, if you are presenting (anything no matter how minor you might believe the subject matter to be), for that time, on that one subject, you are a leader of thought. People will have paid money or time or will have forgone other activities to attend upon you; they may have been obliged to attend upon you, but whatever the reason, it's a major investment by them in you.

No magic wand will improve your speeches. In order to appeal to the noblest and finest sentiments within your audience (and never, ever assume that your watchers and listeners won't understand what you're talking about), your speeches must be filled with allusions to the greatest characters, events, and artistic expressions of the past as well as the present. Know local history, personal history, family history, company history, corporate history, political history, national history, and international history. And know what's current in the world of pop, rock, TV soaps, theater, musicals, opera, movies, literature, religion (be careful), geography, science, current events, the world's conflicts, who's winning what, who's who in the world of sports, what world leaders are thinking, and what the world is thinking about its leaders. Don't simply frequent blogs, e-mails, Web sites, and media sources that support your views. A great orator must be aware of the counterarguments your critics will raise, and he or she must be equipped to deftly address and defuse them. Be clear and logical in your argument.

Passion doesn't have to hide truth or accuracy. Any hint of hypocrisy or cant will sink even the most eloquent speech. Be sincere and show sincerity, not the falsehoods of some politics and business, but real commitment to your subject. If you think what you're talking about is silly or pointless, then it's likely that this will show; the audience will think it's silly or pointless too, and more to the point, they'll think you're a fool. If you snigger at the fact that you have to present sales figures in which you don't believe, or that you have to speak to the induction team instead of Sally Shoesmith, who can't make it today, then you lose. You may think it's smart to be cynical, a notch on your corporate or political belt, but really it isn't. People listening to you will feel the depth of your commitment and will pay attention far more intently if they feel that you are sincere.

The power of the spoken word is undeniable. At all the great moments in history there are great speeches that influenced or caused a desired and often huge outcome. Great speeches have convinced people of the need to fight injustice, to throw off the chains of poverty or tyranny, and even to give their lives for a worthy (and sometimes unworthy or worthless) cause. Words have drawn some sense from the seemingly senseless. Words have comforted those who have suffered a loss so great that they can't easily engage with reality again. Words have given meaning to small and huge events. Words have helped restore dignity, and words have created solemnity when solemnity was required over any levity. Words have created laughter and kinship. Words have made teamwork work. Words have moved people to risk safety. Words make people cry, make people virtuous or angry. Words change people's lives. Words make people feel patriotic or unpatriotic. Words can cause a wry smile, can make people feel warm, and can explain unpleasant necessities. Words can shape and help understanding. Words can foul the air or make it clear.

With this power comes a responsibility. Remember that there are speakers, good speakers, and great speakers. If you really want to wow people with your rhetoric and persuasion, then you must work for it and at it. Become ready not to make *the* great speech, but *a* great speech, one of many. Great speeches share history and use words that resonate with the majority. Yes, even the speeches that are made at Sally Shoesmith's Wednesday afternoon meetings. While most men or women will never summon troops into battle, debate a political bill, publicly resign a senior job in public life, defend the seemingly indefensible, encourage people to save (or attack) another group of people, or explain why there is nothing left to give but hope, most men or women can be an orator. When a speaking opportunity arises, you can be the one everyone thinks of first. The great myth perpetuated about public speaking is that talent in this area is inherent and cannot be learned. This is nonsense. The great orators of the world, from Cicero to Obama, or Pericles to Oskar Schindler, or Barbara Jordan to Jack Welch, or Mary Fisher to Aung San Suu Kyi followed the art of oratory with resolute single-mindedness. You can make what you say matter and unforgettable. You can appeal to your audience. You can speak like a president. (There, the power of three!) You just have to want to do it.

Cicero's ideal was that any orator should sound and behave like Rome's famous actor Roscius: "When people hear he is to speak, all the benches are taken...When he needs to speak, silence is signaled by the crowd followed by repeated applause and much admiration. They laugh when he wishes, when he wishes they cry." Oh, to have heard either Roscius or indeed Cicero speak, and to have learned what they did and then how they did it! As a rule, today's age of digital and Internet-driven communication is lukewarm to rhetoric, and as bloggers and similar increase in number, lazy impulse is often prized over the rhetorical and oratorical magic that we know can move minds. One might argue that a blog can move minds too but normally only as a support to some rhetoric. But people around the world still like oratory. In countries, governments, businesses, colleges, and schools, great orators are delivering great speeches on a daily basis. We listen, and mostly, we love what we hear. We are gratified, inspired, happy, fulfilled, and satisfied.

Speaking like a president is very much a state of mind. Think the right things, create the right speech, and deliver it superbly. Be passionate. Integrity of personal conviction and belief are vital. Be a persuader; be someone who can convert thinking or at least try. Even if you're making a best man's speech, make it count. An audience wants knowledge, passion, leadership, direction, hope, a sense of shared aspiration, and an idea of what they can do to succeed in something. This applies to a best man's speech as much as it does to a presidential inaugural. If you give an audience some of these things, they'll meet you halfway even if they don't agree with all that you say.

Great communicators aren't born but they become so because they must. Churchill wasn't a speaker who found it easy to "go public" let alone become a great orator. He learned from some of the very best—Oliver Cromwell, the Earl of Chatham (William Pitt the Elder), Edmund Burke, Charles James Fox, Henry Peter Brougham, Thomas Babington Macaulay, and William Ewart Gladstone, as well as the Greeks, the Romans, and some nineteenth-century Americans—studying speeches for the communication of anger or encouragement, for examples of how to let pathos rip and how to mollify, or apologize, and how to urge and create belief. You don't have to be a Churchill. You don't have to be a president. But you *do* want to turn a tide with what you say. Don't you? Next time you present to Sally Shoesmith's team or one like it, turn the tide.

Another Beginning

Wednesday Afternoon, London

Wednesday afternoons didn't usually bode well for Sally Shoesmith. It was her own fault really, she mused, as she walked along the agency's dimly lit corridor, a skinny latte in one hand and a bulging briefcase in the other. The lighting, she thought, delicate as it was, always made people look ill—something the creatives hated, particularly when they'd just returned from an expensive shoot in the Caribbean. This particular Wednesday was wet and miserable, the beginnings of winter, she thought gloomily.

Sally had set up her regular sales meetings to begin at two thirty prompt. She always said that they'd be finished by three thirty, but that rarely happened. To begin with, back when the meetings had started, all members of the team had turned up more or less on time and had stayed for the full hour or so. Now there was always an excuse from two or three, sometimes four, often the same people; and invariably one of the remainder would just have to leave early to do something far more important and for someone far more senior than Sally. So she just had to grin and bear it really. Today, she told herself, she was going to be firmer—firmer with them and firmer with the powers that be. After all, this was a sales and projection meeting and therefore important. Her bosses relied on what Sally called "sales intel." She was an important gear in the agency machine, she told herself.

Today it was Andy's turn to give a presentation on new business opportunities based on some fresh research. Sally Shoesmith liked Andy, and she hoped that there'd be a full complement to listen to the presentation. Andy was reasonably new to the agency, and in his short time had made an impression, a positive version of which was not always easy to achieve. She wasn't very sure yet how he would fare in the long term. Certainly, he had to step up to the plate and present his thinking to the teams throughout the business. Tough luck, really, thought Sally, but presentations were foul, and the wretched PowerPoint kept her up nights.

At twenty past two Sally walked into the meeting room called The Rocket for some unknown reason. Was it, she wondered, because of Stevenson's invention? There were ten of the team members ready and waiting. Sally was surprised at such punctuality—and attendance. The eleventh walked past her in a whoosh as Sally stood at the door. Andy had addressed the group before, but only once, and it was when Sally had been away on a course. "Good afternoon," she said to the room. Everyone mumbled and muttered replies. Some continued to doodle; others drained polystyrene. She looked at Andy, who was standing at the front of the room waiting and smiling nicely. "Hi, Sally," he said. "OK if I start?" "Oh, yes, certainly. No PowerPoint then?" asked Sally, looking slightly concerned at the lack of equipment and papers in front of Andy. "No PowerPoint, no," confirmed Andy. "OK," said Sally. "Off you go, then," she said, turning to the eleven expectant faces. "Off you go," she repeated. Her cell phone rang. She ignored it and then saw who it was. She thought about answering it, pressed the green button, but could only hear some wild noise like cheering and someone saying very clearly: "Good to go." Then a pause followed by the words, "Speak like a president."

Further Reading

"Let us read and let us dance—two amusements that will never do any harm to the world."
Voltaire (1694–1778)

If you consider some of the best ever speeches, the ingredients are plain to see. The speeches are thought through, they are sincere (for the most part), and they are given by great speakers, actors who make us, in the audience, believe that what they have to say is true. What we all look for in many speeches is the telling of a good story. And as someone who might want to be a great speaker, you have to know good stories to gain an understanding of what works, of what makes a good beginning, middle, and end, of what excites, amuses, horrifies, pleases, and gladdens. Look at Ray Bradbury for science fiction, Charles Dickens of course for Victorian England and for superb caricatures and characters, Stephen King for shock and horror, J. D. Salinger for his single classic *The Catcher in the Rye*. Look at O. Henry (real name William Sydney Porter), known for writing short stories with wit and surprising plot twists at the end. His most well-known story is *The Gift of the Magi*, in which a poor, young husband and wife each sell a precious possession in order to buy a Christmas present for the other, but, in doing so, each ends up making the other's gift unusable.

Reading good stories is important if you're going to tell good stories. So, read a little F. Scott Fitzgerald. Fitzgerald was a brilliant American writer of novels and short stories, whose works are evocative of the Jazz Age, a term he coined himself. His greatest two short stories are *Bernice Bobs Her Hair* and *The Diamond as Big as the Ritz*. Then there's Edgar Allan Poe—possibly the most famous English language short story writer. Most people can tell you the story of *The Tell-Tale Heart*, *The Masque of the Red Death*, or *The Pit and the Pendulum*. And look at George Eliot (pen name of Mary Anne Evans), considered by many to be one of the most important novelists of the Victorian era. *Middlemarch* is excellent.

Anton Chekhov was a great Russian storyteller. Any of his short stories are worth a look. Before continuing, it's worth pointing out the obvious—you will have your favorite list of writers and books. You must have, because without reading literature you can't add value to what you say in public. You need the fund of ideas, language, and turns of phrase. My list is random and not by any means definitive or with any caveats other than that the writers are great and the books are all good. But that's a subjective view and you'll have your own. That's good.

So where next? Well, *The Adventures of Huckleberry Finn* by Mark Twain is a must and not just because it is commonly accounted as one of the first Great American Novels. It's also one of the first major American novels ever written using vernacular language, told in the first person by Huckleberry "Huck" Finn, best friend of Tom Sawyer (the hero of three other Mark Twain books). *War and Peace* by Leo Tolstoy tells the story of Russian society during the Napoleonic era. It is usually described as one of Tolstoy's two major masterpieces (the other being *Anna Karenina*) as well as one of the world's greatest novels. *Madame Bovary* by Gustave Flaubert, was attacked for obscenity in Paris by public prosecutors when it was first serialized in 1856, resulting in a trial that naturally made it notorious and the writer reasonably wealthy. The novel focuses on a doctor's wife, Emma Bovary, who has adulterous affairs and lives beyond her means in order to escape the boredom of provincial life. Though the basic plot is rather simple, the novel's true delight lies in its details and descriptions. Details and descriptions can be important in storytelling within a speech. Children like story details; so too do adults.

Labyrinths by Jorge Luis Borges is tough to describe without serious analysis, since he has the power to include in five pages a vast universe of the strange and wonderful. It's a terrific fairy tale but one based in the world of harsh reality. *Fear and Loathing in Las Vegas* by Hunter S. Thompson mixes fact and fiction through surrealist imagery to construct an extraordinary drug and political satire. *Catch-22* by Joseph Heller is possibly the most quoted of all war novels. The book's structure centers on irony and repetition. It's a novel that's not easy to put down, creating as it does curiosity and storytelling at its best. Then there's *Kim*, written in 1900 by Rudyard Kipling, about an Anglo-Irish boy who travels across India. It's a vivid and gripping tale. Another great story by Kipling is *Jungle Book*. *Dr Dolittle*, written in 1920 by Hugh Lofting, is worth reading as a great episodic story full of wonder and make-believe. And have a look at these, all great stories: *Lucky Jim* by Kingsley Amis, *The Bottle Factory Outing* by Beryl Bainbridge, *The Adventures of Augie March* by Saul Bellow, *The History Man* by Malcolm Bradbury, *Don Quixote* by Miguel de Cervantes, *Slouching Towards Kalamazoo* by Peter De Vries, *A Fairy Tale of New York* by J. P. Donleavy, *Joseph Andrews* and *Tom Jones* by Henry Fielding, *Cold Comfort Farm* by Stella Gibbons, *The Wind in the Willows* by Kenneth Grahame, *Our Man in Havana* and *Travels with My Aunt* by Graham Greene, *The Little World of Don Camillo* by Giovanni Guareschi, *I Served the King of England* by Bohumil Hrabal, *Three Men in a Boat* by Jerome K. Jerome, *Cakes and Ale* or *The Skeleton in the Cupboard* by W. Somerset Maugham, *Tales of the City* by Armistead Maupin, *Porterhouse Blue* by Tom Sharpe, *The Expedition of Humphry Clinker* by Tobias Smollett, *The Prime of Miss Jean Brodie* by Muriel Spark, *The Life and Opinions of Tristram Shandy, Gentleman* by Laurence Sterne, *Thank You, Jeeves* by P. G. Wodehouse, *The Secret Adversary* by Agatha Christie, *The Woman in White* and *The Moonstone* by Wilkie Collins, *A Study in Scarlet* by Arthur Conan Doyle, *The Secret Agent* by Joseph Conrad, *The Andromeda Strain* and *Jurassic Park* by Michael Crichton, *Poetic Justice* by Amanda Cross, *The Count of Monte Cristo* by Alexandre Dumas, *The Pledge* by Friedrich

Dürrenmatt, *The Crime of Father Amaro* by José Maria de Eça de Queirós, *The Name of the Rose* by Umberto Eco, *LA Confidential* by James Ellroy, anything by Ian Fleming, including his children's stories (such as *Chitty Chitty Bang Bang*), *The Day of the Jackal* by Frederick Forsyth, *The Talented Mr Ripley* by Patricia Highsmith, *Silence of the Grave* by Arnadur Indridason, *Tinker, Tailor, Soldier, Spy* by John le Carré, *To Kill a Mockingbird* by Harper Lee, *The Bourne Identity* by Robert Ludlum, *The Godfather* by Mario Puzo, *The Blue Room* by Georges Simenon, *The Laughing Policeman* by Maj Sjöwall and Per Wahlöö, *Of Mice and Men* by John Steinbeck, *The Face of Another* by Kobo Abe, *The Death of Virgil* by Hermann Broch, *The Vagabond* by Sidonie-Gabrielle Colette, *My Family and Other Animals* by Gerald Durrell, *Silence* by Shusaku Endo, *Howards End* by E. M. Forster, *The Old Man and the Sea* by Ernest Hemingway, *The Ambassadors* by Henry James, *One Flew Over the Cuckoo's Nest* by Ken Kesey, *Cider with Rosie* by Laurie Lee, *The Assistant* by Bernard Malamud, *The God of Small Things* by Arundhati Roy, *The History of Mr Polly* by H. G. Wells, *To the Lighthouse* by Virginia Woolf, *Dom Casmurro* by Joaquim Maria Machado de Assis, *Beauty and Sadness* by Yasunari Kawabata, *Zorba the Greek* by Nikos Kazantzakis, *Of Human Bondage* by Somerset Maugham, *Doctor Zhivago* by Boris Pasternak, *The Graduate* by Charles Webb, *The Hitchhiker's Guide to the Galaxy* by Douglas Adams, *Childhood's End* by Arthur C. Clarke, *Dune* by Frank Herbert, *Brave New World* by Aldous Huxley, *The Unconsoled* by Kazuo Ishiguro, *The Chronicles of Narnia* by C. S. Lewis, *Nineteen Eighty-Four* by George Orwell, *Titus Groan* by Mervyn Peake, *His Dark Materials* by Philip Pullman, *Harry Potter and the Philosopher's Stone* by J. K. Rowling, *Frankenstein* by Mary Shelley, *The Hobbit* by J. R. R. Tolkien, *The Midwich Cuckoos* by John Wyndham, *We* by Yevgeny Zamyatin, *She: A History of Adventure* by H. Rider Haggard, *On the Road* by Jack Kerouac, *Moby Dick* by Herman Melville, *The Cruel Sea* by Nicholas Monsarrat, *The Virginian* by Owen Wister, *The Caine Mutiny* by Herman Wouk.

Well, that's a few and certainly enough to be going on with. It's up to you. And I make no apology for recommending these books. They are all superb in their own way and they each mean a great deal to me. Anyway, whether for the purpose of gleaning ideas or better understanding language and argument, reading them or some of them will do you no harm.

Not all the great speakers in the world were great readers, of course. But, now, to make a mark on stage and to become a great speaker, you have to read, not just novels of course, but newspapers and magazines, Web site research and blogs. Children's stories and fairy tales from all over the world are worth reading too. They are often, in equal measure, very funny, wicked, vicious, and caring. Hans Christian Andersen is a good source as are the stories of the brothers Jacob and Wilhelm Grimm. Shakespeare is one of the best storytellers (possibly the best).

Further Reading for Speechmakers

In terms of reading specifically about speeches and speech craft, the following are useful:

Cicero and D. H. Berry (translator). *Defence Speeches*. Oxford Paperbacks, 2008.*

Clinton Bill, Mary Frances Berry and Josh Gottheimer. *Ripples of Hope*. Basic Civitas Books, 2003.

Crystal, Prof David. *Making Sense of Grammar*. Longman, 2004.

Daley, James (editor). *Great Speeches by African Americans: Frederick Douglass, Sojourner Truth, Dr. Martin Luther King, Jr., Barack Obama, and Others*. Dover Thrift Editions, 2006.

DiNunzio, Mario. *Woodrow Wilson: Essential Writings and Speeches of the Scholar-president*. New York University Press, illustrated edition, 2006.

---

* A wonderful example of an opening gambit: "Holding as I do, Cato, a very high opinion of your moral standards, I could not possibly fault your judgement; but there are perhaps a few respects in which I could shape and improve it slightly."

Gallo, Carmine. *The Presentation Secrets of Steve Jobs: How to Be Insanely Great in Front of Any Audience*. McGraw-Hill Professional, 2009.

Johnson Brian K. and Marsha Hunter. *Articulate Advocate: New Techniques of Persuasion for Trial Lawyers (Articulate Life)*. Crown King Books, 2009.

MacArthur, Brian. *The Penguin Book of Historic Speeches*. Penguin, 1996.

Mandela, Nelson. *Selected Speeches and Writings of Nelson Mandela: The End of Apartheid in South Africa*. Red and Black Publishers, 2010.

Matthews, Brander. *Notes on Speech-Making*. BiblioBazaar, 2010.

Mukherjee, Rudrangshu (editor). *Great Speeches of Modern India*. Random House India, 2010.

Oates, Stephen B. *With Malice Toward None: The Life of Abraham Lincoln* HarperPerennial; reprint edition, 1994.

Obama, Barack. *The Audacity of Hope: Thoughts of Reclaiming the American Dream*. Crown/Three Rivers Press, 2006.[†]

Obama, Barack. *Dreams from My Father: A Story of Race and Inheritance*. Times Books, 1995.

Obama, Barack and ObamaQuotes.com. *Inspire a Nation: Barack Obama's Most Electrifying Speeches of the 2008 Election (International edition): Includes Obama's Berlin Speech and Election Night Victory Speech*. Publishing 180, 2008.

Roosevelt, Franklin D. *My Friends: Twenty-eight History Making Speeches*. Foster & Stewart Publishing Corp, 1945.

Ryan, Halford R. (editor). *The Inaugural Addresses of Twentieth-century American Presidents*. Praeger Series in Political Communication, Greenwood Press, 1993.

[†]   The phrase "the audacity of hope" came from Obama's 2004 Democratic National Convention keynote address: "I'm talking about something more substantial. It's the hope of slaves sitting around a fire singing freedom songs; the hope of immigrants setting out for distant shores; the hope of a young naval lieutenant bravely patrolling the Mekong Delta; the hope of a millworker's son who dares to defy the odds; the hope of a skinny kid with a funny name who believes that America has a place for him, too. Hope in the face of difficulty. Hope in the face of uncertainty. The audacity of hope!"

Safire, William. *Lend Me Your Ears: Great Speeches in History*. W. W. Norton & Co, 2nd revised edition, 1997.

Slayden, Dr. David and Dr. Rita Kirk Whillock. *Soundbite Culture: the Death of Discourse in a Wired World*. Sage Publications, Inc; illustrated edition, 1999.

Timmerman, David M. and Edward Schiappa. *Classical Greek Rhetorical Theory and the Disciplining of Discourse*. Cambridge University Press, 2010.

And some great listening:

William Jefferson Clinton: Great Speeches (Audio CD), Soundworks, US (2002)

Never Give In! No 1: Winston Churchill's Greatest Speeches (Audio CD), BBC Audiobooks Ltd (2005)

The Greatest Speeches of All-Time Vol.III (Audio CD), SpeechWorks (2007)

The Greatest Speeches of All Time: Includes President Barack Obama's Inaugural Address (Audio CD), Phoenix Books (2009)

This Is Your Moment: Inspirational Commencement Speeches (Audio CD), Phoenix Books (2010)

Yes We Can! Speeches of Barack Obama (Audio CD), Hachette Audio (2009)

My Fellow Americans with 2 CDs: The Most Important Speeches of America's Presidents, from George Washington to George W. Bush (Audio CD) by Michael Waldman, Sourcebooks Mediafusion; Har/Com edition (2003)

US Presidents 1929–2008 3 Vols: Original Speeches from 13 Presidents of the United States (Audio CD), Soundworks Inc. (2008)

Talking Heads: Great Speeches from the First Century of Recorded Sound (Audio CD), Chrome Dreams (2001)

Index